PHILIPPIANS

THE
TEACHER'S
OUTLINE & STUDY
BIBLE

PHILIPPIANS

THE

TEACHER'S

OUTLINE & STUDY

BIBLE

NEW TESTAMENT

KING JAMES VERSION

Leadership Ministries Worldwide
PO Box 21310
Chattanooga, TN 37424-0310

Please address all requests for information or permission to:
Leadership Ministries Worldwide
PO Box 21310
Chattanooga TN 37424-0310
Ph.# 615-855-2181 FAX # 615-855-8616 CompuServe # 74152,616

Library of Congress Catalog Card Number: 94-073070
International Standard Book Number: 0-945863-37-3

PRINTED IN THE U.S.A.

PUBLISHED BY LEADERSHIP MINISTRIES WORLDWIDE

H O W   T O   U S E

THE TEACHER'S OUTLINE AND STUDY BIBLE (TOSB)

To gain maximum benefit, here is all you do. Follow these easy steps, using the sample outline below.

1 STUDY TITLE

2 MAJOR POINTS

3 SUB-POINTS

**4 COMMENTARY, QUES-
TIONS, APPLICATION,
ILLUSTRATIONS**
(Follows Scripture)

1. First: Read the **Study Title**
two or three times so that
the subject sinks in.
2. Then: Read the **Study Title**
and the **Major Points** (Pts.1,2,3)
together quickly. Do this
several times and you will
quickly grasp the overall subject.
3. Now: Read both the **Major Points**
and **Sub-Points**. Do this slower
than Step 2. Note how the points

B. The Steps to Peace (Part II): Prayer & Positive Thinking, 4:6-9	
1. Peace comes through prayer	6 Be careful for nothing; but in every thing by prayer and supplication with thanksgiving
a. The charge: Do not worry or be anxious	
b. The remedy: Prayer	
1) About everything	let your requests be
2) With requests	made known unto
3) With thanksgiving	God.
c. The promise: Peace	7 And the peace of
1) Peace that passes all understanding	God, which passeth all understanding, shall
2) Peace that keeps our hearts & minds	keep your hearts and minds through Christ Jesus.
2. Peace comes through positive thinking	8 Finally, brethren, whatsoever things are true, whatsoever
a. The charge: Think & practice things that are...	things are honest, whatsoever things are
1) True	just, whatsoever
2) Honest	things are pure,
3) Just	whatsoever things
4) Pure	are lovely, what-

are beside the applicable verse, and simply state what the Scripture is saying—in Outline
form.
4. Read the **Commentary**. As you read and re-read, pray that the Holy Spirit will bring to your
attention exactly what you should study and teach. It's all there, outlined and fully
developed, just waiting for you to study and teach.

<u>TEACHERS, PLEASE NOTE:</u>

⇒ Cover the **Scripture** and the **Major Points** with your students. Drive the **Scripture** and
Major Points into their hearts and minds.

(Please continue on next page)

i

⇒ Cover *only some of the commentary* with your students, not all (unless of course you have plenty of time). Cover only as much commentary as is needed to get the major points across.

⇒ Do NOT feel that you must...
- cover all the commentary under each point
- share every illustration
- ask all the questions

An abundance of commentary is given so you can find just what you need for...
- your own style of teaching
- your own emphasis
- your own class needs

PLEASE NOTE: It is of utmost importance that you (and your study group) grasp the Scripture, the Study Title, and Major Points. It is this that the Holy Spirit will make alive to your heart and that you will more likely remember and use day by day.

MAJOR POINTS include:

APPLICATIONS:
Use these to show how the Scripture applies to everyday life.

ILLUSTRATIONS:
Simply a window that allows enough light in the lesson so a point can be more clearly seen. A suggestion: Do not just "read" through an illustration if the illustration is a story, but learn it and make it your own. Then give the illustration life by communicating it with *excitement & energy*.

QUESTIONS:
These are designed to stimulate thought and discussion.

A CLOSER LOOK
In some of the studies, you will see a portion boxed in and entitled: "A Closer Look." This discussion will be a closer study on a particular point. It is generally too detailed for a Sunday School class session, but more adaptable for personal study or an indepth Bible Study class.

PERSONAL JOURNAL
At the close of every lesson there is space for you to record brief thoughts regarding the impact of the lesson on your life. As you study through the Bible, you will find these comments invaluable as you look back upon them.

Now, may our wonderful Lord bless you mightily as you study and teach His Holy Word. And may our Lord grant you much fruit: many who will become greater servants and witnesses for Him.

REMEMBER!

The Teacher's Outline & Study Bible is the only study material that actually outlines the Bible verse by verse for you right beside the Scripture. As you accumulate the various books of The Teacher's Outline & Study Bible for your study and teaching, you will have the Bible outlined book by book, passage by passage, and verse by verse.

The outlines alone makes saving every book a must! (Also encourage your students, if you are teaching, to keep their student edition. They also have the unique verse by verse outline of Scripture in their version.)

Just think for a moment. Over the course of your life, you will have your very own personalized commentary of the Bible. No other book besides the Bible will mean as much to you because it will contain your insights, your struggles, your victories, and your recorded moments with the Lord.

"Study to show thyself approved unto God, a workman that needeth not to be ashamed, rightly dividing the word of truth" (2 Tim.2:15).

"All scripture is given by inspiration of God, and is profitable for doctrine, for reproof, for correction, for instruction in righteousness: that the man of God may be perfect, throughly furnished unto all good works" (2 Tim.3:16-17).

*** All direct quotes are followed by a Superscript Endnote number. The credit information for each Endnote is listed at the end of the individual study session for your reference.

MISCELLANEOUS ABBREVIATIONS

&	=	And
Bckgrd.	=	Background
Bc.	=	Because
Circ.	=	Circumstance
Concl.	=	Conclusion
Cp.	=	Compare
Ct.	=	Contrast
Dif.	=	Different
e.g.	=	For example
Et.	=	Eternal
Govt.	=	Government
Id.	=	Identity or Identification
Illust.	=	Illustration
K.	=	Kingdom, K. of God, K. of Heaven, etc.
No.	=	Number
N.T.	=	New Testament
O.T.	=	Old Testament
Pt.	=	Point
Quest.	=	Question
Rel.	=	Religion
Resp.	=	Responsibility
Rev.	=	Revelation
Rgt.	=	Righteousness
Thru	=	Through
V.	=	Verse
Vs.	=	Verses

Publisher &
Distributor of...

DEDICATED:

To all the men and women of the world
who study and teach the Gospel of our
Lord Jesus Christ
and
To the Mercy and Grace of God.

• Demonstrated to us in Christ Jesus our Lord.

> "In whom we have redemption through His
> blood, the forgiveness of sins, according to the
> riches of His grace." (Eph. 1:7)

• Out of the mercy and grace of God His Word has
flowed. Let every person know that God will have
mercy upon him, forgiving and using him to fulfill
His glorious plan of salvation.

> "For God so loved the world, that he gave his only
> begotten Son, that whosoever believeth in him should
> not perish, but have everlasting life. For God sent not
> his Son into the world to condemn the world; but that
> the world through him might be saved." (John 3:16-17)

> "For this is good and acceptable in the sight of God
> our Saviour; who will have all men to be saved,
> and to come unto the knowledge of the truth." (I Tim. 2:3-4)

The Teacher's Outline & Study Bible

is written for God's people to use
in their study and teaching of God's Holy Word.

ACKNOWLEDGMENTS

Every child of God is precious to the Lord and deeply loved. And every child as a servant of the Lord touches the lives of those who come in contact with him or his ministry. The writing ministry of the following servants have touched this work, and we are grateful that God brought their writings our way. We hereby acknowledge their ministry to us, being fully aware that there are so many others down through the years whose writings have touched our lives and who deserve mention, but the weaknesses of our minds have caused them to fade from memory. May our wonderful Lord continue to bless the ministry of these dear servants, and the ministry of us all as we diligently labor to reach the world for Christ and to meet the desperate needs of those who suffer so much.

THE GREEK SOURCES

1   Expositor's Greek Testament, Edited by W. Robertson Nicoll. Grand Rapids, MI: Eerdmans Publishing Co., 1970

2.   Robertson, A.T. Word Pictures in the New Testament. Nashville, TN: Broadman Press, 1930.

3.   Thayer, Joseph Henry. Greek-English Lexicon of the New Testament. New York: American Book Co.

4.   Vincent, Marvin R. Word Studies in the New Testament. Grand Rapids, MI: Eerdmans Publishing Co., 1969.

5.   Vine, W.E. Expository Dictionary of New Testament Words. Old Tappan, NJ: Fleming H. Revell Co.

6.   Wuest, Kenneth S. Word Studies in the Greek New Testament. Grand Rapids, MI: Eerdmans Publishing Co.

THE REFERENCE WORKS

7.   Cruden's Complete Concordance of the Old & New Testament. Philadelphia, PA: The John C. Winston Co., 1930.

8.   Josephus' Complete Works. Grand Rapids, MI: Kregel Publications, 1981.

9.   Lockyer, Herbert, Series of Books, including his Books on All the Men, Women, Miracles, and Parables of the Bible. Grand Rapids, MI: Zondervan Publishing House.

10. Nave's Topical Bible. Nashville, TN: The Southewstern Co.

11. The Amplified New Testament. (Scripture Quotations are from the Amplified New Testament, Copyright 1954, 1958, 1987 by the Lockman Foundation. Used by permission.)

12. The Four Translation New Testament (Including King James, New American Standard, Williams - New Testament In the Language of the People, Beck - New Testament In the Language of Today.) Minneapolis, MN: World Wide Publications.

13. The New Compact Bible Dictionary, Edited by T. Alton Bryant. Grand Rapids, MI: Zondervan Publishing House, 1967.

14. The New Thompson Chain Reference Bible. Indianapolis, IN: B.B. Kirkbride Bible Co., 1964,

THE COMMENTARIES

15. Barclay, William. Daily Study Bible Series. Philadelphia, PA: Westminister Press.

16. Bruce, F.F. The Epistle to the Ephesians. Westwood, NJ: Fleming H. Revell Co., 1968.

17. Bruce, F.F. Epistle to the Hebrews. Grand Rapids, MI: Eerdmans Publishing Co., 1964.

18. Bruce, F.F. The Epistles of John. Old Tappan, NJ: Fleming H. Revell Co., 1970.

19. Criswell, W.A. Expository Sermons on Revelation. Grand Rapids, MI: Zondervan Publishing House, 1962-66.

20. Green, Oliver. The Epistles of John. Greenville, SC: The Gospel House, Inc., 1966.

21. Green, Oliver. The Epistles of Paul the Apostle to the Hebrews. Greenville, SC: The Gospel House, Inc., 1965.

22. Green, Oliver. The Epistles of Paul the Apostle to Timothy & Titus. Greenville, SC: The Gospel House, Inc., 1964.

23. Green, Oliver. The Revelation Verse by Verse Study. Greenville, SC: The Gospel House, Inc., 1963.

24. Henry, Matthew. Commentary on the Whole Bible. Old Tappan, NJ: Fleming H. Revell Co.

25. Hodge, Charles. Exposition on Romans & on Corinthians. Grand Rapids, MI: Eerdmans Publishing Co., 1972-1973.

26. Ladd, George Eldon. A Commentary On the Revelation of John. Grand Rapids, MI: Eerdmans Publishing Co., 1972-1973.

27. Leupold, H.C. Exposition of Daniel. Grand Rapids, MI: Baker Book House, 1969.

28. Newell, William R. Hebrews, Verse by Verse. Chicago, IL: Moody Press.

29. Strauss, Lehman. Devotional Studies in Philippians. Neptune, NJ: Loizeaux Brothers.

30. Strauss, Lehman. Galatians & Ephesians. Neptune, NJ: Loizeaux Brothers.

31. Strauss, Lehman. The Book of the Revelation. Neptune, NJ: Loizeaux Brothers.

32. The New Testament & Wycliffe Bible Commentary, Edited by Charles F. Pfeiffer & Everett F. Harrison. New York: The Iverson Associates, 1971. Produced for Moody Monthly. Chicago Moody Press, 1962.

33. The Pulpit Commentary, Edited by H.D.M. Spence & Joseph S. Exell. Grand Rapids, MI: Eerdmans's Publishing Co., 1950.

34. Thomas, W.H. Griffith. Hebrews, A Devotional Commentary. Grand Rapids, MI: Eerdman's Publishing Co., 1970.

35. Thomas, W.H. Griffith. Studies in Colossians & Philemon. Grand Rapids, MI: Baker Book House, 1973.

36. Tyndale New Testament Commentaries. Grand Rapids, MI: Eerdman's Publishing Co., Began in 1958.

37. Walker, Thomas. Acts of the Apostles. Chicago, IL: Moody Press, 1965.

38. Walvoord, John. The Thessalonian Epistles. Grand Rapids, MI: Zondervan Publishing House, 1973.

OTHER SOURCES

39. Barna, George. The Frog In The Kettle. Ventura, CA: Regal Books, 1990. Used by Permission.

40. Bright, Dr. Bill. Witnessing Without Fear. San Bernardino, CA: Here's Life Publishers, 1987.

41. Bryant, David. In the Gap. Ventura, CA: Regal Books, 1981. Used by Permission.

42. Doan, Eleanor. The Speaker's Sourcebook. Grand Rapids, MI: Zondervan Publishing House, 1971. Used by permission of Zondervan Publishing House.

43. Graham, Billy. Peace With God. Dallas, TX: Word Publishing, 1953.

44.   Hughes, R. Kent. Disciplines of a Godly Man. Wheaton, IL: Crossway Books, 1991.

45.   Hybels, Bill. Honest to God? Grand Rapids, MI: Zondervan Publishing House, 1990. Used by permission of Zondervan Publishing House.

46.   Knight, Walter B. Three Thousand Illustrations for Christian Service. Grand Rapids, MI: Eerdmans Publishing Company, 1971.

47.   Larson, Craig B., Editor. Illustrations for Preaching and Teaching. Grand Rapids, MI: Baker Books, 1993.

48.   McGee, J. Vernon. Thru The Bible, 5 Vols.. Nashville, TN: Thomas Nelson Publishers, 1983.

49.   Morley, Pat. The Rest of Your Life. Nashville, TN: Thomas Nelson Publishers, 1992.

50.   Smalley, Gary & Trent, Dr. John. Giving The Blessing: Daily Thoughts On The Joy Of Giving. Nashville, TN: Thomas Nelson Publishers, 1993.

51.   Wiersbe, Warren W. The Bible Exposition Commentary, Vol.2. Wheaton, IL: Victor Books, 1989.

LEADERSHIP MINISTRIES WORLDWIDE

OUR FIVEFOLD MISSION & PURPOSE:

● To share the Word of God with the world.

● To help the believer, both minister and layman alike, in his understanding, preaching, and teaching of God's Word.

● To do everything we possibly can to lead men, women, boys, and girls to give their hearts and lives to Jesus Christ and to secure the eternal life which He offers.

● To do all we can to minister to the needy of the world.

● To give Jesus Christ His proper place, the place which the Word gives Him. Therefore — No work of Leadership Ministries Worldwide will ever be personalized.

This material, like similar works, has come from imperfect man and is thus susceptible to human error. We are nevertheless grateful to God for both calling us and empowering us through His Holy Spirit to undertake this task. Because of His goodness and grace, *The Preacher's Outline & Sermon Bible™* - New Testament is complete in 14 volumes as well as the single volume of **The Minister's Handbook**.

God has given the strength and stamina to bring us this far. Our confidence is that, as we keep our eyes on Him and grounded in the undeniable truths of the Word, we will continue working through the Old Testament Volumes and on the new, forthcoming series (1995) *The Teacher's Outline & Study Bible.* Future materials will include CD-ROM, The Believer's *Outline* Bible, and similar *Outline* and **Handbook** materials.

To everyone, everywhere who preaches and teaches the Word, we offer this material firstly to Him in whose name we labor and serve, and for whose glory it has been produced.

Our daily prayer is that each volume will lead thousands, millions, yes even billions, into a better understanding of the Holy Scriptures and a fuller knowledge of Jesus Christ the incarnate Word, of whom the Scriptures so faithfully testify.

As you have purchased this volume, you will be pleased to know that a portion of the price you paid goes to underwrite providing similar volumes at affordable prices in other languages (Russian, Korean, Spanish and others yet to come) to a preacher, pastor, church leader, or Bible student somewhere around the world, who will present God's message with clarity, authority, and understanding beyond their own. *Amen.*

For ministry information, prices and shipping details, kindly contact:

LEADERSHIP MINISTRIES WORLDWIDE

P.O. Box 21310, 515 Airport Road, Suite 107
Chattanooga, TN 37424-0310
(615) 855-2181 FAX (615) 855-87616
CompuServe: 74152,616

> **"**
> *Go ye therefore, and*
> *teach all nations*
> **"** (Mt. 28:19)

OUTLINE OF PHILIPPIANS

THE TEACHER'S OUTLINE & STUDY BIBLE is *unique*. It differs from all other Study Bibles and Teaching Materials in that every Passage and Subject is outlined right beside the Scripture. When you choose any *Subject* below and turn to the reference, you have not only the Scripture, but you discover the Scripture and Subject *already outlined for you--verse by verse*.

For a quick example, choose one of the subjects below and turn over to the Scripture--you will find this to be a marvelous help for faster, easier, and more meaningful study of Scripture. *In addition, every point* of the Scripture and Subject is *fully developed in a Commentary with* these Unique Features: Personal Application, Illustrations, Questions, and much more! Again, this arrangement makes study preparation much easier and faster.

A suggestion: For the quickest overview of Philippians, first read *all the major titles* (I, II, III, etc.), then come back and read the subtitles.

OUTLINE OF PHILIPPIANS

THE EPISTLE OF PAUL THE APOSTLE TO THE

PHILIPPIANS

INTRODUCTION

AUTHOR: Paul, the Apostle.

Clement of Rome, who lived in the first century, wrote a letter to the Corinthians and referred to Paul's letter to the Philippians. Polycarp, who lived in the second century, wrote the Philippians and mentioned Paul's letter. Ignatius, another early church leader, alluded to it. There are other references to Paul's authorship by Irenaeus, Clement of Alexandria, and Tertullian--all early church writers (Ralph P. Martin. *The Epistle of Paul to the Philippians*. "Tyndale Bible Commentaries," ed. by RVG Tasker. Grand Rapids, MI: Eerdmans, 1959, p.28, 36).

DATE: Uncertain. Probably somewhere around A.D. 60-63 while Paul was in prison at Rome.

TO WHOM WRITTEN: "To all the saints in Jesus Christ which are at Philippi, with the bishops and deacons" (Ph.1:1). The message is applicable to all the saints of every church.

PURPOSE: Paul wrote Philippians for several reasons.

1.   He wished to prevent any criticism against a very dear friend and servant of Christ, Epaphroditus. Epaphroditus had been sent by the Philippian church to deliver a gift and to encourage Paul while he was a prisoner in Rome. But Epaphroditus became extremely sick, almost to the point of death, while with Paul. His return to Philippi was delayed, apparently for a long time. Because of this, Paul feared criticism of Epaphroditus by the church. They might think he was a weakling or a quitter. So Paul wrote to ease the path for Epaphroditus and to prevent any criticism of him (Ph.2:25-30).

2.   Paul wished to thank the Philippian church for its help throughout his ministry. They had sent him a gift right after he had founded the church and moved on (Ph.1:5; 4:15; 2 Cor.8:1f). They had also sent gifts to him at Thessalonica (Ph.4:16) and at Corinth (2 Cor.11:9). And now they sent him not only a gift, but even more, a dear, dear believer to minister to his needs while he was in prison (Ph.2:25-30; 4:18).

3.   Paul wished to call the church to unity and harmony. There were two ladies who quarreled and were causing a disturbance (Ph.4:2; cp. 1:27; 2:2-4, 14). It was this disturbance that called forth one of the greatest pictures of Christ in the Holy Scriptures (Ph.2:5-11).

4.   Paul wished to deal with some false teachers who were just beginning to arise in the church (Ph.3:2f).

SPECIAL FEATURES:

1.   The City of Philippi. Philippi was the gateway to Europe. It lay on the great Roman road known as the Egnatian Way. The city was named after Philip of Macedonia, the father of Alexander the Great. The site was a natural fortress, sitting on a range of hills that separated Europe from Asia, the East from the West. The city was a strategic center commanding the great Egnatian Way.

Philippi was also a proud Roman colony. In fact, it was famous as a miniature Rome. A city became a Roman colony in one of two ways. At first Rome founded colonies throughout the outer reaches of the Empire to keep the peace and to guard against invasions from barbaric hordes. Veteran soldiers, ready for retirement, were usually granted citizenship if they would go out and settle these colonies. Later on, however, a city was granted the distinctive title of a Roman Colony for loyalty and service to the Empire. The distinctive thing about these colonies was their fanatic loyalty to Rome. The citizens kept all their Roman ties, the Roman language, titles, customs, affairs, and dress. They refused to allow any infiltration of local influence whatsoever. They totally rejected the influence of the world around them. They were Roman colonists within an alien environment.

The city of Philippi fit right into Paul's master plan. Its strategic location on the Egnatian Way assured the spread of the gospel throughout the Roman Empire. As Paul carried on his ministry, he was moving toward Rome and the regions beyond into Spain. He knew that the converts from Philippi, whose employment took them from Philippi throughout the Empire, could move on out ahead of him. The strong witness of businessmen and other new converts could reach the world for Christ far greater than he could by himself (cp. Acts 28:13f).

2. The Church at Philippi. Acts 16:1-40 describes the founding of the Philippian church on Paul's second missionary journey. It is one of the most exciting adventures in all of literature. Philippi witnessed the entrance of the gospel into Europe. Paul had made several attempts to go elsewhere, but the Holy Spirit prohibited him (Acts 16:6-7). Thus, he made his way to Troas, not really knowing why. While in Troas Paul experienced the incredible vision of a man in Macedonia crying out, "Come over and help us." Through that one vision, the Holy Spirit changed the cradle of society. He thrust Paul forth into Europe with the glorious gospel of Christianity, and since that day, the world has never been the same.

From Troas, Paul landed at the European or Macedonian port of Neapolis and immediately made his way to the strategic city of Philippi. When Paul arrived in Philippi he found what he called "a crooked and perverse generation" (Ph.2:15). He also found a small nucleous of women who had a Jewish background to which he could appeal. From this group there were two significant conversions: Lydia, a prominent business woman, and an unnamed slave girl who was possessed with a spirit of fortune-telling. Later on there was also a Roman jailer and his household who were converted. Paul was soon attacked and imprisoned and forced to leave Philippi. Consequently, the church had only a small beginning under Paul's personal leadership.

When Paul left, Luke remained with the handful of converts (Acts 17:1). The church met at Lydia's house and continued to grow (Acts 16:40). The converts came primarily from the pagan Gentile world (Ph.2:25; 4:2-3; Ro.15:26-27).

The strength of the Philippian church is seen in the fact that the church continued to support Paul throughout his ministry despite the little time he had with them. They supported him even while they themselves were suffering and being persecuted (cp. Ph.1:7, 27-30; 2:15; 3:10-11; 4:1). No wonder Paul called them "brethren dearly beloved and longed for, my joy and crown" (Ph.4:1) and boasted of them to other churches (2 Cor.8:1f).

3. Philippians is "The Most Personal of Paul's Epistles." It is written to a church dearly loved by the minister (cp. Ph.4:1).

4. Philippians is "The Epistle of Stewardship" (see Purpose, point 2).

5. Philippians is "The Epistle of Joy." The words "joy" and "rejoicing" are used sixteen times in four short chapters.

6. Philippians is "The Epistle That Stresses the Little Phrase 'In Christ' or 'In the Lord'." The whole thesis of Paul is that life is "*in Christ*" and that Christ is to be "*in life*" (cp. Ph.1:13, 14, 26, 29; 2:1, 5, 19, 24, 29; 3:1, 4, 9, 14; 4:1, 4, 6-7, 10, 13, 17, 21).

THE EPISTLE OF PAUL THE APOSTLE TO THE

PHILIPPIANS

	I. THE MARKS OF GOD'S PEOPLE, 1:1-30 **A. The Marks of a Healthy Church, 1:1-2** **CHAPTER 1**
1. A healthy church disciples young people **2. A healthy church serves Christ** **3. A healthy church is full of true saints** **4. A healthy church has leaders who lead by example** **5. A healthy church experiences grace & peace**	Paul and Timotheus, the servants of Jesus Christ, to all the saints in Christ Jesus which are at Philippi, with the bishops and deacons: 2 Grace be unto you, and peace, from God our Father, and from the Lord Jesus Christ.

Section I
THE MARKS OF GOD'S PEOPLE, Philippians 1:1-30

Study 1: **THE MARKS OF A HEALTHY CHURCH**

Text: **Philippians 1:1-2**

Aim: To do all you can to help build a healthy church.

Memory Verse:
> "Grace be unto you, and peace, from God our Father, and from the Lord Jesus Christ" (Ph.1:2).

INTRODUCTION:
When you take a picture with your camera, it takes time for the film to develop. If you have an instamatic camera, you can see your picture develop right before your very eyes. At first glance, that picture looks pretty unimpressive—just a white square. But in a matter of moments, form and color begin to appear. Shapes become more distinctive and the color sharpens. In a few minutes, the subject of your attention has been captured on film, an eyewitness record of what has been seen.

In the same sense, every church needs time to develop into a healthy church. Some churches develop faster than others for a variety of reasons. As you look at your own church, do not become discouraged if it appears to be only an unimpressive white square of blank film. Christ has made an eternal commitment to the church until it becomes fully mature. Look closely, and you will begin to see Him bring shape and color—a glorious maturity—to the Church.

What are those shapes and colors that display a picture of a healthy church? Paul will show us as we study this text.

15

This is a most unusual greeting to a church from Paul. He does not refer to himself as an apostle of Jesus Christ. Why? There was no need for him to defend his call from God. His relationship with the church at Philippi was just what it should be: a relationship founded and rooted in Jesus Christ and in the love and respect for each other. The church held its minister, Paul, close to its heart; they loved and cared for him as few churches love and care for their ministers. This greeting gives some outstanding distinctives of a healthy church.

OUTLINE:
1. A healthy church disciples and nurtures young people (v.1).
2. A healthy church serves Christ (v.1).
3. A healthy church is full of true saints (v.1).
4. A healthy church has leaders who lead by example (v.1).
5. A healthy church experiences grace & peace (v.2).

1. A HEALTHY CHURCH DISCIPLES AND NURTURES YOUNG PEOPLE (v.1).

In the words "Paul and Timothy" we see a *father and son in the faith*—the adult and the young person together. There was deep affection that bound Paul and Timothy together. That affection found its root and purpose in the mission of the Lord Jesus Christ. Paul contributed the wisdom of experience, and Timothy the hope and vibrant energy of youth. It should be noted that the adult, Paul, is mentioned first. The adult always holds the primary responsibility and privilege for taking hold of young people and making disciples of them. This was the command of the Lord's *great commission*; therefore, the believer must always keep his focus upon finding young people and making disciples of them.

> "And the things that thou hast heard of me among many witnesses,
> the same commit thou to faithful men, who shall be able to teach others
> also" (2 Tim.2:2).

QUESTIONS:
1. Who has been your "Paul," your spiritual mentor? In one sentence, describe what kind of impact that person made on your life.
2. Are you discipling and nurturing a new believer in Christ? If not, who could you be discipling? Some family member? Some fellow church member? Some fellow worker?

2. A HEALTHY CHURCH SERVES CHRIST (v.1).
Believers are slaves of Jesus Christ. The word "servant" is the word *bond-slave* in Greek. There is a distinct difference between a servant and a slave. A servant is free to work for whomever he wishes; a slave is bought and purchased—completely and totally owned by a master. A slave is bound by law to his master.

Paul calls himself and Timothy the *slaves of Jesus Christ*. A look at the slave market of Paul's day shows more clearly what Paul meant when he said he was a "slave of Jesus Christ."
1. The slave was owned and totally possessed by his master. This is what Paul meant. Paul was purchased and possessed by Christ. Christ had looked upon him and had seen his degraded and needful condition. And when Christ looked, the most wonderful thing happened: Christ loved him and bought him. Therefore, he was now the possession of Christ.
2. The slave existed for his master and no other reason. He had no personal rights whatsoever. The same was true with Paul: he existed only for Christ.
3. The slave served his master and existed only for the purpose of service. He was at the master's disposal any hour of the day. So it was with Paul: he lived only to serve Christ—hour by hour and day by day.
4. The slave's will belonged to his master. He was allowed no will and no ambition of his own. He was completely subservient to the master and owed total obedience to the will of the

master. Paul belonged to Christ. In fact, he even said that he fought and struggled to bring *every thought* into captivity "to the obedience of Christ" (2 Cor.10:3-5, esp. 5).

5.   There is a fifth and most precious thing that Paul meant by his being "a slave of Jesus Christ." He meant that he had the highest and most honored and kingly profession in all the world. Men of God, the greatest men of history, have always been called "the servants of God." It was the highest title of honor. The believer's slavery to Jesus Christ is no cringing, cowardly, or shameful subjection. It is the position of honor—the honor that bestows upon a man the privileges and responsibilities of serving the King of kings and Lord of lords.

APPLICATION:

The great need today is for men and women to become *slaves* of the Lord Jesus Christ. We must become His slaves and do what He says. Then and only then will the world be reached with the glorious news of eternal life. Then and only then will the desperate needs of the world be met.

> "If any man serve me, let him follow me; and where I am, there shall also my servant be: if any man serve me, him will my Father honour" (Jn.12:26; cp. Ro.12:1; 1 Cor.15:58).

ILLUSTRATION:

How many of you have ever "burned-out" on serving? If you have, you might be able to relate to this story. Listen closely:

> *"Burnout. Was this my reward for giving so much to so many people? I volunteered for every committee duty. 'Teach a Sunday school class? Sure, and I'll help with vacation Bible school as well.'*
>
> *I thought that serving in a civic club would relieve me of the guilt I felt for not caring for the poor as I should. I was sure that my efforts would be praised by many. 'We can change the hearts of men if we work hard and get the right politicians in office.' Or so I thought. I worked hard for those people and only got a generic post-card thanking me for my vote!*
>
> *Well, I've had it! From now on, I'm going to do my own thing and forget about serving other people. So many of them are ungrateful anyway, no matter how much I do."*

Oswald Chambers has some words of wisdom for those who relate to this story:

> *"If we are devoted to the cause of humanity, we shall soon be crushed and brokenhearted...but if our motive is love for God, no ingratitude can hinder us from serving our fellow men."*

QUESTIONS:

1. In what area of your life do you have the hardest time becoming a slave of Jesus Christ? Why?
2. What differences would there be in your life if every area of your life were enslaved to Him?
3. What differences would there be in your church—in the Christian body as a whole—if we were all enslaved to Him?

3. A HEALTHY CHURCH IS FULL OF TRUE SAINTS (v.1).

All believers—true believers—are called *saints*. The Bible never uses the word *saint* to refer to a few people in the church who have achieved unusual spiritual maturity. The word *saints* refers to the *sanctified or holy ones*. It simply means to be set apart and to be separated. Therefore, every believer who has truly trusted Jesus Christ as his Savior is separated from the world and set apart to live for God. Every true believer is a "saint," a person set apart unto God. There are three stages of sanctification.

PHILIPPIANS 1:1-2

1. *There is initial or positional sanctification.* When a person believes in Christ, he is immediately set apart for God—once and for all—permanently. He is set apart—positioned—to live for God day by day.

> **"By the which will we are sanctified through the offering of the body of Jesus Christ once for all" (Heb.10:10).**

2. *There is progressive sanctification.* The true believer makes a determined and disciplined effort to allow the Spirit of God to set him apart day by day. The Spirit of God takes him and conforms him into the image of Christ more and more—for as long as he walks upon this earth. The believer grows and progresses in maturity more and more day by day.

> **"But we all, with open face beholding as in a glass the glory of the Lord, are changed into the same image from glory to glory, even as by the Spirit of the Lord" (2 Cor.3:18).**

3. *There is eternal sanctification.* The day is coming when the believer will be perfectly set apart unto God and His service—without any sin or failure whatsoever. That day will be the great and glorious day of the believer's eternal redemption.

> **"That he might present it to himself a glorious church, not having spot, or wrinkle, or any such thing; but that it should be holy and without blemish" (Eph.5:27).**

APPLICATION:
We are the property of the Lord Jesus, set apart as His holy possession. We should live as the possession of the Lord. We should walk as the separated people of God, living holy and righteous lives.

In light of all that God has done for us, how can we do anything less than to live a sanctified, holy life before God? How can we be lethargic and complacent, sleepy-eyed, and unmotivated? How can we allow ourselves to live lives of routine and unconcern? How can we live lives of indulgence, license, selfishness, immorality, perversion, wickedness, and evil?

> **"But the day of the Lord will come as a thief in the night; in the which the heavens shall pass away with a great noise, and the elements shall melt with fervent heat, the earth also and the works that are therein shall be burned up. Seeing then that all these things shall be dissolved, what manner of persons ought ye to be in all holy conversation [behavior] and godliness, looking for and hasting unto the coming of the day of God, wherein the heavens being on fire shall be dissolved and the elements shall melt with fervent heat?" (2 Pt.3:10-12).**

QUESTIONS:
1. To whom does the word "saint" refer when it is used in the Bible? Are there people who go to church who are not saints?
2. What kinds of things are keeping you from being sanctified, from being conformed to God's image?

4. A HEALTHY CHURCH HAS LEADERS WHO LEAD BY EXAMPLE (v.1).

Note that both bishops and deacons are mentioned as being in the Philippian church. What Paul is doing is addressing the leaders of the church and setting them apart from the membership whom he addressed as "saints." The point to see in this passage is that believers organize for ministry.

1. The bishops were apparently the same as the elders or ministers of a church. The two words are used interchangeably to refer to the same men. The bishop was the person whom we call the minister or pastor of the church.

2. The deacons were spiritually minded men who had dedicated their lives to the Lord to minister to the *saints* of God. They were persons who were chosen to minister to the widows and widowers and to the poor and sick of a church *in order to free the minister to concentrate on prayer and preaching*. But note a significant fact:

⇒ Preachers are sometimes called deacons, that is servants.

> "Who then is Paul, and who is Apollos, but ministers [diakonoi] by whom ye believed, even as the Lord gave to every man?" (1 Cor.3:5).

⇒ The first deacons preached as well as ministered to the needy of the church.

> "And Stephen [a deacon], full of faith and power, did great wonders and miracles among the people" (Acts 6:8).
> "Then Philip [a deacon] went down to the city of Samaria, and preached Christ unto them" (Acts 8:5).

APPLICATION:
Two significant points need to be stressed.
1. The church must organize for ministry and must always be careful to ordain only persons who have proven to be spiritually mature in the Lord.
2. The two ordained officers of the church must be diligent in both their duty and in sharing the Word of the Lord. Every believer is needed to bear witness for the Lord Jesus, and the *leadership must take the lead*. How can we expect others to be witnessing and ministering if the leadership is not doing so?

> "But so shall it not be among you: but whosoever will be great among you, shall be your minister: and whosoever of you will be the chiefest, shall be servant of all" (Mk.10:43-44).

QUESTIONS:
1. What are some responsibilities of church leaders?
2. Are popularity, financial wealth, and political power important qualifications for church leadership? Explain your answer.
3. What qualities should a leader in the church have in order to serve?
4. Think of your church leaders (pastors, elders, deacons, teachers, etc.). Are they setting the example in leadership?
5. Do you pray for your church leaders by name? Would you be willing to make a commitment to do so now? Would you commit to a few minutes of prayer each day for your church leaders, staff, and missionaries?

5. A HEALTHY CHURCH EXPERIENCES GRACE AND PEACE (v.2)

The minister, Paul, wanted the believers of Philippi to experience the grace and peace of God and of the Lord Jesus Christ.

1. Grace means the *undeserved favor and blessings* of God. The word *undeserved* is the key to understanding grace. Man does not deserve God's favor; he cannot earn God's approval and blessings. God is too high and man is too low for man to deserve anything from God. Man is imperfect and God is perfect; therefore, man cannot expect anything from God. Man has re

PHILIPPIANS 1:1-2

acted against God too much. Man has...

- rejected God
- rebelled against God
- ignored God
- neglected God
- cursed God

- sinned against God
- disobeyed God
- denied God
- questioned God

Man deserves nothing from God except judgment, condemnation, and punishment. But God is love—perfect and absolute love. Therefore, God makes it possible for man to experience His grace, in particular the favor and blessing of salvation which is in His Son, Jesus Christ.

"In whom we have redemption through his blood, the forgiveness of sins according to the riches of his grace" (Eph.1:7).

2.   Peace means to be bound together with God and with everyone else. It means to be secure in the love and care of God. It means to have a knowledge that God will...

- provide
- guide
- save

- deliver
- encourage
- strengthen

- sustain
- give real life both now and forever

A person can experience true peace only as he comes to know Jesus Christ. Only Christ can bring peace to the human heart, the kind of peace that brings deliverance and assurance to the human soul.

"Peace I leave with you, my peace I give unto you: not as the world giveth give I unto you. Let not your heart be troubled, neither let it be afraid" (Jn.14:27).

The point is this: not everyone in the church was experiencing the grace and peace of God. Some were church members, but they had never trusted Christ to save them, not really. They depended upon their own works and goodness to make them acceptable to God. As a result they did not have peace of heart. Some had even fallen into all forms of sin and shame. Others had become extremely critical and divisive, standing against Paul and any who supported Paul (Ph.1:27; 2:1-4; 3:3, 18-19; 4:2). Paul just wished the very best for the church of Philippi. He wanted all—every single member—to experience...

- the grace of God by coming to know Jesus Christ as their personal Lord and Savior.
- the peace of God as they walked through life confronting all its struggles and trials.

APPLICATION:
Church members must guard against making a false profession of Christ, guard against trusting their own works and goodness to save them and to make them acceptable to God. We must all make sure that we have experienced the grace and peace of our Lord Jesus Christ.

ILLUSTRATION:
D.L. Moody, a famous evangelist of a former day, made this statement while preaching:

"It is well that man cannot save himself; for if a man could...work his own way to Heaven, you would never hear the last of it. Why, if a man happens to get a little ahead of his fellows and scrapes a few thousand...dollars together, you'll hear him boast of being a self-made man. I've heard so much of this sort of talk that I am sick and tired of the whole business; and I am glad that...in Heaven we will never hear anyone bragging of how he worked his way to get there."

20

1. Have you personally experienced the grace and peace of God? Have you truly trusted Jesus Christ as your Savior?
2. Are you lacking God's peace in any area of your life? If your answer is yes, how can your lack of peace be resolved?
3. What practical things can you do to share the grace and peace of God with people?
4. Who do you know that needs to be touched by God's grace and peace?

SUMMARY

As we have gone through this study, we have seen the foundations of a healthy church getting a little bit clearer. Just remember, as it takes time for the shapes and colors of a picture to develop, it takes time for a church to develop into a healthy church. Pray for your church and give yourself to its mission by getting involved and by living out these five important points:
1. Nurture and disciple young people.
2. Be a slave of Jesus Christ.
3. Live as a saint should live.
4. Be a leader who leads by example.
5. Make sure you have truly experienced God's grace and peace and become a vessel of God's grace and peace to others.

PERSONAL JOURNAL NOTES
(Reflection & Response)

1. The most important thing that I learned from this lesson was:

2. The area that I need to work on the most is:

3. I can apply this lesson to my life by:

4. Closing Statement of Commitment:

---

[1]Oswald Chambers. Quoted in *The Speaker's Sourcebook* by Eleanor Doan. (Grand Rapids, MI: Zondervan Publishing Company, 1971), p.224.
[2]From *Mid-Continent*. Quoted in *Three Thousand Illustrations for Christian Service* by Walter B. Knight (Grand Rapids, MI: Eerdmans Publishing Company, 1971), p.326.

	B. The Marks of Mature Believers, 1:3-11	bonds, and in the defence and confirmation of the gospel, ye all are partakers of my grace.	c. Partners in the gospel d. Partners in grace e. Partners with Christ
1. The mark of a thankful heart	3 I thank my God upon every remembrance of you,	8 For God is my record, how greatly I long after you all in the bowels of Jesus Christ.	
2. The mark of prayer	4 Always in every		
3. The mark of joy	prayer of mine for you all making request with joy,	9 And this I pray, that your love may abound yet more and more in	7. The mark of a growing & discerning love
4. The mark of fellowship	5 For your fellowship in the gospel from the first day until now;	knowledge and in all judgment;	
5. The mark of confidence in God's salvation a. Is a good work b. Is incomplete c. Is to be completed at Christ's return	6 Being confident of this very thing, that he which hath begun a good work in you will perform it until the day of Jesus Christ:	10 That ye may approve things that are excellent; that ye may be sincere and without offence till the day of Christ;	a. To approve the excellent b. To live pure lives c. To cause no one to stumble
6. The mark of partnership a. Partners in heart b. Partners in suffering	7 Even as it is meet for me to think this of you all, because I have you in my heart;· inasmuch as both in my	11 Being filled with the fruits of righteousness, which are by Jesus Christ, unto the glory and praise of God.	8. The mark of righteousness

Section I
THE MARKS OF GOD'S PEOPLE, Philippians 1:1-30

Study 2:   THE MARKS OF MATURE BELIEVERS

Text: Philippians 1:3-11

Aim: To honestly measure your own spiritual maturity.

Memory Verse:
    "Being confident of this very thing, that He which hath begun a good work in you will perform it until the day of Jesus Christ" (Ph.1:6).

INTRODUCTION:
    A tape measure is a must when you need an accurate measurement. How long is that bolt that you need? About 4 inches? Maybe 5? If you need one that is exactly 4 inches, you'll need an exact measurement. A random measurement is not effective when you need to be precise.
    Do you live your life randomly? Have you measured your maturity in Christ accurately? A random measurement is not good enough. The Bible teaches us that we are to measure our spiritual maturity.

    What are the marks of a mature Christian believer? What are the marks of a dynamic, mature Christian church? This passage answers these questions. Concisely and clearly, the marks so desperately needed by believers and churches are spelled out.

OUTLINE:
1. The mark of a thankful heart (v.3).
2. The mark of prayer (v.4).
3. The mark of joy (v.4).
4. The mark of fellowship (v.5).
5. The mark of confidence in God's salvation (v.6).
6. The mark of partnership (v.7-8).
7. The mark of a growing and discerning love (v.9-10).
8. The mark of righteousness (v.11).

1. THE FIRST MEASURING MARK: A THANKFUL HEART (v.3).

Paul did not stand alone in the world. He was not the only person living for God and sharing Christ. He belonged to a great family, a family of believers who constituted the family of God. They, too, were living for God and sharing Christ with a lost and needful world. Remember that Paul was in prison in Rome and that he was a great distance from the Philippian believers. He did not have their presence; all he had was the memory of their time together. And sitting there in prison, remembering their love and care and support, his heart swelled up with thanksgiving for them, and he thanked God for them.

APPLICATION:
What a lesson for us! If Paul, in such dark circumstances, thanked God for believers who were so far away from him, how much more should we thank God for each other. We have the love and care and support of each other week by week and day by day, and we can call upon each other for help any hour of any day. Yet how often do we thank God for each other?

Another point is this: we should be following Paul's example, thanking God for all believers every day. We are not alone in the world. God is building a body of people world-wide—a body of people who are just like us—committed to live for the Lord Jesus Christ and to carry His gospel of salvation and love and care to a world that reels under the weight of desperate need.

> "Giving thanks unto the Father, which hath made us meet to be par-
> takers of the inheritance of the saints in light" (Col.1:12).

ILLUSTRATION:
How can you have a thankful heart?

Picture a balance scale with a bowl attached to each side. Now picture this same scale inside your heart. On the left side of the scale the bowl quickly fills up with the various trials of the day: worries, misunderstandings, hurt feelings, financial stress—just to name a few.

It just seems that life is not fair. Your scale has become too weighted with bad things.

A mature believer knows how to bring a balance to life's problems. How? By deciding to fill the bowl on the right with a THANKFUL HEART. No one ever said that it would be easy or that all of your circumstances had to be pleasant.

A THANKFUL HEART comes from two things: asking and trusting God for the strength to bear the trials of life, and deliberately choosing to give thanks. As the believer acts in faith, God comes and fills his heart with an overflowing strength and gratitude.

QUESTIONS:
1. Why is it so difficult to give thanks during unpleasant circumstances? How can you prepare your heart ahead of time to be thankful?
2. Who is the most thankful person that you know? What makes them so thankful?
3. Are you thankful for: salvation? family? friends? church? When was the last time you thanked God for each of these? (Start a list of things you are thankful for and add to it daily. You will quickly tip the scale in favor of blessings!)

2. THE SECOND MEASURING MARK: PRAYER (v.4).

Paul says that he always prayed for the church. The idea is that he prayed all throughout the day for them. They were constantly on his mind and in his prayers.

APPLICATION:
What a dynamic lesson in prayer for us: To pray by name throughout the day for all the churches we know! We tend to pray for our own church (sometimes) and forget about the other churches that are such a vital part of the Lord's work!

Our prayer life must be consistent. How many of us pray as we should?! We must pray as if we really believe that prayer changes things and not just when we get around to it.

> **"For God is my witness, whom I serve with my spirit in the gospel of his Son, that without ceasing I make mention of you [the Roman church] always in my prayers" (Ro.1:9).**

(Keep in mind that Paul had never even seen the Roman church. He had only heard of their faith and witness for Christ!)

QUESTIONS:
1. Would you consider your prayer life as:
   a) full-time b) part-time c) not working at the moment
2. What can you do right now to make improvements in your prayer life?

Suggestion: Just as you make a list of things to be thankful for, also make a list of things to pray for. Then make a commitment to the Lord to pray every day for those things. Add to it. Be faithful. Now, as you make your prayer list, ask yourself such questions as these:
   a. When should I pray?
   b. Where can I get alone to pray?
   c. Who do I need to pray for?
   d. What things and situations should be in my prayers?
   e. What does the Bible tell me to pray for? Pray for...
   - Ministers (1 Th.5:25)
   - Those who are in authority (1 Tim.2:1-3)
   - The afflicted (Jas.5:13)
   - One another (Jas.5:16)
   - The lost (Ro.10:1)
   - God's will (Mt.6:10)
   - Your daily bread (Mt.6:11)
   - Deliverance from temptation (Mt.6:13)
   - Good things (Mt.7:11)

3. THE THIRD MEASURING MARK: JOY (v.4).

Remember that Paul is in prison, yet his heart is filled with joy. Joy means an inner gladness; a deep seated pleasure. It is a depth of assurance and confidence that ignites a cheerful and rejoicing heart. It is a cheerful heart that leads to cheerful and rejoicing behavior.

The joy of the Lord is not the same as the joy of the world. The joy of the world is more of a temporary pleasure than joy. The world's joy is always nagged by some incompleteness, some missing ingredient. There is not a not a complete sense of assurance, confidence, and satisfaction. There is the knowledge that something can go wrong: circumstances can change or some situation can arise to disturb the joy (sickness, death, financial loss, war). The *haunting awareness* always keeps the world's joy from being full and complete, assuring and satisfying.

Several things need to be said about the believer's joy.

1.   *Joy is divine.* It is possessed and given only by God. Its roots are not in earthly or material things or cheap triumphs. It is the joy of the Holy Spirit, a joy based in the Lord. It is His very own joy (Jn.15:11).

2.   *Joy does not depend on circumstances or happiness.* Happiness depends upon happenings, but the joy that God implants in the believer's heart overrides all, even the matters of life and death (Ps.5:11).

3.   *Joy springs from faith* (Ro.15:13).

4.   *Joy of future reward makes and keeps the believer faithful* (Heb.12:2).

The source of the believer's joy is severalfold.
- ⇒ The fellowship of the Father and His Son brings joy (1 Jn.1:3-4).
- ⇒ Victory over sin, death, and hell brings joy (Jn.14:28).
- ⇒ Repentance brings joy (Lk.15:7).
- ⇒ The hope of glory brings joy (Ro.14:17).
- ⇒ The Lord's Word—the revelations, commandments, and promises which He made—brings joy (Jn.15:11).
- ⇒ The commandments of Christ and the will of God bring joy. Obeying and doing a good job stirs joy within the believer's heart (Jn.17:13).
- ⇒ Prayer brings joy (Jn.16:24).
- ⇒ The presence and fellowship of believers brings joy (1 Jn.1:3-4).
- ⇒ Converts bring joy (1 Th.2:19-20).
- ⇒ Hearing that others walk in the truth brings joy (3 Jn.1:4).
- ⇒ Giving brings joy (Heb.10:34).

> **"Thou wilt show me the path of life: in thy presence is fulness of joy;**
> **at thy right hand there are pleasures for evermore" (Ps.16:11).**

QUESTIONS:
1. Do you sometimes allow the happiness of worldly things to replace the true joy of the Lord?
2. Do you ever allow the small disappointments in life to rob you of the joy of the Lord? What are some examples?
3. How can you change your focus to the things that are truly important in life, the things that bring true joy and that are eternal?

4. THE FOURTH MEASURING MARK: FELLOWSHIP (v.5).

Note two significant points.

1.   The source of fellowship is the gospel of the Lord Jesus Christ, the great salvation of God. The gospel of Christ is the glorious news that He has died for our sins, risen again, and conquered death that we might live with God eternally, never having to die (cp. 1 Cor.15:3). Christian believers have a spiritual bond and *fellowship* because...
- they have experienced the *same salvation*, the salvation of God.
- they have embraced the *same faith.*

Genuine believers are to live and proclaim the gospel. They are to serve and bear witness to the same Lord; therefore, their lives are bound together in the Spirit of Christ and His fellowship.

2.   The fellowship of believers is to exist from the very first day of salvation. What a glorious testimony the Philippian church had! It had been about ten years since some of the members had given their lives to follow Christ and had founded the church. And note: the fellowship of the church had continued from the very first day of its founding. As all churches experience, there must have been differences and problems which had arisen, but the believers handled them *in Christ*—just as they should have. Therefore, the peace and unity of the Spirit was kept alive and the fellowship of the church remained strong.

APPLICATION:
One of the most critical needs facing the church today is the need for peace and unity in the Spirit of God—a strong fellowship rooted around the gospel of Christ. This doesn't mean just singing, eating, and socializing together. It means praying together...
- with friends
- with family
- with congregations
- with Bible Study groups
- with Sunday School classes & departments
- with converts

"For where two or three are gathered together in my name, there am I in the midst of them" (Mt.18:20).

ILLUSTRATION:
Becoming a part of a *church fellowship* will expand your life. In the following quote, David Bryant challenges the church to unite for the cause of world missions.

"World missions cannot happen without a vital, growing, global community of disciples who burn with the fire of a world vision. Christians aren't meant to be a collection of spectators....We're not to sit by passively waiting for the Kingdom to suddenly materialize before our eyes. The Church is the agent of God's world-wide purpose. We're to be more like a caravan of ambassadors, going forth to bless the families of the earth, than a royal entourage basking in the sunlight of God's love for us."[1]

QUESTIONS:
1. What are some of the opportunities you have to participate in the fellowship of your church?
2. What kinds of things hinder you from committing yourself to more fellowship?
3. What are some examples of unity that you have noticed in your church fellowship? What were the results of this fellowship?

5. THE FIFTH MEASURING MARK: AN UNSHAKEN CONFIDENCE IN GOD'S SALVATION (v.6).

God will complete His good work in believers. Confidence and assurance are two of the striking traits of genuine believers. Believers know God personally. God's Spirit actually lives within the heart and body of the believer (Jn.14:16). The Spirit of God actually bears witness with the spirit of the believer, that he is going to be redeemed someday—presented perfect before God. In fact, the presence of the Holy Spirit within the believer's body is the guarantee of the believer's salvation (2 Cor.1:22).
1. *The believer has absolute confidence in the work of salvation which God has begun in his life.*
2. *The work begun by God is a good work*; that is, it is a work that revolutionizes or radically changes the life of the believer.
3. *The good work is incomplete as long as the believer lives on this earth.* He is never perfected, not while a man. There is always work for God to do.
4. *The good work is to be completed when Jesus Christ returns to this earth.* At that time, the believer will be transformed into a perfect man and given a perfect body. And he will worship and serve the Lord Jesus in perfection throughout all eternity.

"I know whom I have believed, and am persuaded that he is able to keep that which I have committed unto him against that day" (2 Tim.1:12).

26

APPLICATION:

As believers we can take heart! God is not finished with us yet!

Think of a sculptor who begins a project with a block of clay. Each day he pinches and prods away to reveal what he sees inside the shapeless form. He knows all along what the end product will be, but no one else does!

Likewise we are like clay in God's hands. He continues to mold us day by day, always working with us, sometimes having to patch up the cracks, holes, and dents we have made in His creation. But if we have given our lives to God—truly believed and trusted Him to save us—we can have confidence:

⇒ God will save us—not toss us aside.
⇒ God's work in us is good—not for any evil purpose.
⇒ God's work is continuous: He is still working in us and on us!
⇒ God's work will be completed and perfected only when Jesus Christ returns. We shall be conformed to the image of Christ more and more day by day, but we shall never be perfected, not until Christ returns. We must always remember this.

6. THE SIXTH MEASURING MARK: PARTNERSHIP (v.7-8).

Paul and the church were so closely bound together that they formed a partnership.

1. *They were partners in heart.* Paul loved them as he loved himself; he held them ever so dear to his heart and they constantly filled his thoughts.

2. *They were partners in the sufferings of Paul.* This means...
   • that they were sympathizing with Paul in his imprisonment.
   • that they were sending hope to Paul while he was in prison.
   • that they had or were themselves suffering because of the gospel just as Paul was.

The point is this: the affection between Paul and the Philippians was so tender that their hearts went out to each other. What one experienced, the other felt, even the sufferings of each other.

> **"We then that are strong ought to bear the infirmities of the weak, and not to please ourselves" (Ro.15:1).**

ILLUSTRATION:
Are you regularly in tune with the needs of other people around you?

> *"Jackie Robinson was the first black [man] to play major league baseball. While breaking baseball's color barrier, he faced jeering crowds in every stadium.*
> *"While playing one day in his home stadium in Brooklyn, he committed an error. His own fans began to ridicule him. He stood at second base, humiliated, while the fans jeered.*
> *"Then shortstop 'Pee Wee' Reese came over and stood next to him. He put his arm around Jackie Robinson and faced the crowd. The fans grew quiet. Robinson later said that arm around his shoulder saved his career."[2]*

Who needs your arm around their shoulder today?

3. *They were partners in the gospel.* They were actively defending and proclaiming the truth of the gospel, actively bearing witness to the saving grace of the Lord Jesus Christ. They were taking the great commission of our Lord seriously.

"Go ye therefore, and teach all nations, baptizing them in the name of
the Father, and of the Son, and of the Holy Ghost: teaching them to observe all things whatsoever I have commanded you: and, lo, I am with you
alway, even unto the end of the world" (Mt.28:19-20).

4.   *They were partners in the grace of God.* Paul and the Philippian church were expressing
the wonderful favor and blessings of God. God was pouring the richest blessings upon both Paul
and the church. Why? What was it that caused God to so richly bless these two? Their faithfulness: as this passage shows, they were bearing the marks of mature believers.

"In whom we have redemption through his blood, the forgiveness of
sins, according to the riches of his grace" (Eph.1:7).

5.   *They were partners with Christ.* It was the tenderness—the tender mercies, compassion,
and deep affection—of Jesus Christ that Paul had for the Philippians. He longed for them with
the very affection and tenderness of Christ Himself.

APPLICATION:
The minister and church desperately need such tenderness and affection for each other!
What a tremendous difference would exist in churches if believers held each other so ten-
derly—held each other with the tenderness and affection of Christ Himself.
The great need of the church today is for partnership—partnership among its members.
Believers desperately need to become partners with each other and with the minister of
God:
⇒   partners in heart
⇒   partners in suffering
⇒   partners in proclaiming and defending the gospel
⇒   partners in the grace of God
⇒   partners with the Lord Jesus Christ

"A new commandment I give unto you, That ye love one another; as I
have loved you, that ye also love one another. By this shall all men know
that ye are my disciples, if we have love one to another" (Jn.13:34-35).

QUESTIONS:
1. How would you characterize your current Christian experience?
   a.   a solo—singing a lot by yourself
   b.   a duet—you've been doing music with only one other person
   c.   an ensemble—singing with a small group of friends
   d.   a community choir—you sing your part, but don't stand out; your absence is not
        noticed.
2. What are some ways you can get involved and become a partner in your church? With
   your minister?
3. What qualities do you like to seek when forming a partnership?

7. THE SEVENTH MEASURING MARK: A GROWING AND DISCERNING LOVE (v.9-10).

Note this: love in the Bible never focuses upon *good feelings*. Feelings may and usually do
come to the person who truly loves another person, but feelings are never the focus—not with
true love. What then is the focus?
⇒   The *focus* of love is knowledge. If we truly love someone, we want to know all we can
    about the person.

⇒ The *force* of love is judgment. The word means intelligence or discernment. If we truly love someone, we want to learn all we can about the person. We want to gather all the intelligence and facts possible, discerning them so that we can please the person.

There are three reasons why we need a love that grows more and more.

1. *A growing love is needed to strive for things that are excellent.* It is not enough just to know what is right and wrong. It is not enough just to do what is right. Sometimes the choice is between the good and the excellent, the acceptable and the best. Only a *growing love* will stir us to choose the excellent and the best.

⇒ The more we love the Lord, the more we will choose the excellent and best for Him.

⇒ The more we love each other, the more we will choose the excellent and best for each other. A growing love will not want to do anything that would even come close to causing a person to stumble.

2. *A growing love is needed to be sincere and pure.* The word *sincere* means to sift about through a sieve in order to make pure. Therefore, the word means pure and uncontaminated. We are to stay pure until the return of Christ. Only a growing love will keep our eyes focused upon Christ. If we do not love Him, we will not look to Him. If we love Him, we will keep our eyes fastened upon Him, longing to see and be with Him. Only true love will keep us pure while waiting for His return.

3. *A growing love is needed to keep us from causing others to stumble.* We must always guard against being an offense or a stumblingblock to others. Note: we must be willing to choose the best and the excellent for the sake of others. We may be able to control, but others may not be able to control...

- drinking
- television
- movies
- dancing

- eating
- social functions
- heavy makeup that attracts attention

- the latest fashion and dress that exposes the body

The list could go on and on with almost everything we do. We must control everything we do, not slipping over into the questionable—sometimes not even doing the acceptable and good, but we must choose the best. Approve only the things that are excellent. Why?

⇒ To keep from causing a brother to stumble.

⇒ To offer up to the Lord the very best we can. This point should *break our hearts.* Just think how often we have chosen to do less than the best for our Lord. We have offered up to Him behavior, words, thoughts, deeds, works that were second best—and we knew it! How His heart must have been cut—especially when He went to the ultimate limit in loving and giving Himself for us.

"And he said to them all, If any man will come after me, let him deny himself, and take up his cross daily, and follow me" (Lk.9:23).

QUESTIONS:
1. Why do we need to have a growing and discerning love?
2. On what should your focus be? Why is this important?
3. What are some excellent things that you need to strive for today?
4. At this moment, would you consider your love to be:
   a. a growing love
   b. a struggling love
   c. a lukewarm love

8. THE EIGHTH MEASURING MARK: RIGHTEOUSNESS (v.11).

What does righteous mean? It means *acting right.* But Scripture declares a shocking fact: there are none righteous, except Jesus Christ. Therefore, the believer's heart is to be focused upon the Lord Jesus Christ and His righteousness, and that focus must be protected. It is not enough to let the righteousness of Christ cover us. The Christian must protect his heart by living as righteously as he can. Righteousness keeps the heart from losing its focus.

The Christian believer is to...
- strive after the very righteousness of Jesus Christ: believe with all his heart that the righteousness of Jesus Christ covers him and makes him acceptable to God.
- live righteously in this present world.

"For He hath made Him to be sin for us, who knew no sin; that we might be made the righteousness of God in Him" (2 Cor.5:21).

QUESTIONS:
1. What practical things can you do to guard your heart?
2. What kinds of things will interfere with living righteously?
3. Can you bear fruit if you do not try to live righteously? Why?

SUMMARY:

Every Christian believer can measure his spiritual maturity by looking at these marks within his life:
1. A thankful heart
2. A consistent prayer life
3. A heart and life full of joy
4. A strong fellowship with other believers
5. An unshaken confidence in God's salvation
6. A partnership with other Christian believers
7. A growing and discerning love
8. A life of righteousness

PERSONAL JOURNAL NOTES:
(Reflection & Response)

1. The most important thing that I learned from this lesson was:

2. The area that I need to work on the most is:

3. I can apply this lesson to my life by:

4. Closing Statement of Commitment:

---

[1]David Bryant, *In the Gap* (Madison, WI: Inter-Varsity Missions, 1981), p.109-110.
[2]Craig B. Larson, Editor, *Illustrations For Preaching and Teaching* (Grand Rapids, MI:Baker Books, 1993), p.144.

	C. The Marks of a Mature & Active Witness, 1:12-19	and strife, and some also of good will:	for credit or prestige

1. He shares the gospel regardless of circumstances
a. Paul faced dark circumstances: He was a prisoner in Rome
b. Paul used his dark circumstances to spread the gospel
  1) Spread through the elite guard of Rome: In the palace & everywhere else
  2) Spread by encouraging believers to be more fearless witnesses
2. He holds no personal jealousy nor desire
	12 But I would ye should understand brethren, that the things which happened unto me have fallen out rather unto the furtherance of the gospel; 13 So that my bonds in Christ are manifest in all the palace, and in all other places; 14 And many of the brethren in the Lord, waxing confident by my bonds, are much more bold to speak the word without fear. 15 Some indeed preach Christ even of envy	16 The one preach Christ of contention, not sincerely, supposing to add affliction to my bonds: 17 But the other of love, knowing that I am set for the defence of the gospel. 18 What then? notwithstanding, every way, whether in pretence, or in truth, Christ is preached; and I therein do rejoice, yea, and will rejoice. 19 For I know that this shall turn to my salvation through your prayer, and the supply of the Spirit of Jesus Christ,	a. Others preached Christ with jealous & contentious spirits, hoping to cause trouble for Paul
			b. Still others preached in love, supporting Paul
			
			c. Paul rejoiced in this one thing: Christ was being preached-- whether from false motives or true, Christ was preached
			3. He possesses the assurance of a happy ending: Salvation
			a. Through prayer
			b. Through the Holy Spirit

Section I
THE MARKS OF GOD'S PEOPLE, Phillipians 1:1-30

Study 3: **THE MARKS OF A MATURE AND ACTIVE WITNESS**

Text: Philippians 1:12-19

Aim: To become a mature and active witness for Christ.

Memory Verse:
"For we cannot but speak the things which we have seen and heard" (Acts 4:20).

INTRODUCTION:
Do you ever get a little nervous when you have to share your faith? Do you get butterflies in your stomach? You are not alone in feeling that way. How many times have you promised God that you would learn how to share your witness, only to put it off until another more opportune time? Dr. Bill Bright says:

"Witnessing is an activity we frequently shrink from. To intrude in someone else's life seems not only threatening but blatantly presumptuous. We fear offending the other person, fear...being rejected, fear...doing an inadequate job of representing our Lord and even being branded a 'fanatic.' So we remain silent, and pray that God will use someone else to get His message to those around us who do not know Him."[1]

Sound familiar? As we shall soon see, Paul has the antidote for the fear of witnessing!

OUTLINE:
1. He shares the gospel regardless of circumstances (v.12-14).
2. He holds no personal jealousy nor desire for credit or prestige (v.15-18).
3. He possesses the assurance of a happy ending: salvation (v.19).

1. A MATURE WITNESS SHARES THE GOSPEL REGARDLESS OF THE CIRCUM-STANCES (V.12-14).

Note two significant points.

1.   Paul faced dark circumstances: he was a prisoner in Rome, waiting to appear before the Supreme Court. He was facing a trial before Nero, the Roman Emperor, and he was innocent. He had done nothing that should have caused his arrest and imprisonment. Yet there he was, and he was having to await the arrival of his Jewish prosecutors with their trumped-up, malicious charges. True, he had some privileges—renting his own house and receiving friends—but these privileges were minor when the strains of his sufferings are seen. He was imprisoned for over two years, and as is the case with all prisoners, the days wore on ever so slowly—hour by hour and day after day. His life was hanging in the balance. As Paul says in Eph.3:13, his tribulations were intense and drawn out.

But note something: Paul...
*   did not grumble and complain
*   did not question God and wonder why
*   did not whine and murmur
*   did not fall to pieces
*   did not curse God nor give up his faith

2.   Paul used his dark circumstances to spread the gospel. Paul did not see himself as a prisoner of Rome nor of Nero. He saw himself as a prisoner *for Jesus Christ*. He did not see himself as a victim; he saw himself as a conqueror *for Jesus Christ*. In Acts 28:20 Paul says he was "bound with this chain," and in Eph.6:20 he calls himself an "ambassador in bonds." The word "halusis" is used. The "halusis" was a small length of chain that bound a prisoner to the wrist of a guard to prevent his escape. Just imagine! Paul was bound to a Roman guard every day and night for over two years. What do you suppose Paul talked about with the guards? He tells us: "The things which happened to me have fallen out to the futherance of the gospel."
  a.   *Paul spread the gospel through the Praetoria Guard*, the *elite* of the Roman army. These soldiers guarded and were chained to the wrist of Paul day and night for two years. How many Paul led to the Lord is unknown. But note: Christ was shared so much that the gospel spread throughout...
*   the whole Praetorian guard (16,000 of them).
*   the palace of the emperor.
*   all other places.

Paul—through his imprisonment and stand for Christ and the gospel which he preached—became the conversation throughout Rome, the conversation among all the social circles including the upper strata, the very palace of the emperor himself.

ILLUSTRATION:
How can we live such a victorious life in Christ, a life so victorious that it conquers even the most terrible circumstances?

"The superintendent of a mission school read the text, 'My yoke is easy.' Turning to the children she asked, 'Who can tell me what a yoke is?' A little girl said, 'Something they put on the necks of animals.' Then she inquired, 'What is the meaning of God's yoke?' All were silent for a moment, when the hand of a four-year-old child went up and she said, 'God putting his arms around our necks.' What could be more comforting than that?" [2]

PHILIPPIANS 1:12-19

APPLICATION:
   The lesson for us is this: we must never let circumstances get us down—never let them defeat our testimony and witness for Christ, no matter what they are...

- persecution
- accident
- failure
- financial loss
- rejection

- bankruptcy
- sin
- abuse
- divorce
- poverty

- imprisonment
- age
- loss of a loved one

If we are living for Christ, we must *know* that God is in control of our lives. He will strengthen us to bear whatever circumstances fall upon us. We must use the circumstances to witness to the saving power of Christ—to the eternal hope He gives of forgiveness and of living forever. We must witness to all around us when we...

- lie in the bed of sickness
- are in the midst of death
- are facing money problems
- are being abused and persecuted

And if we have sinned and failed—no matter how terribly—we must repent and get back to the task of witnessing, overcoming the circumstances of having failed and sinned so much. We must do all we can to conquer the circumstances for Christ and continue to witness, sharing all the good we can in order to reach all we can. All must be done for Christ, for He is worthy. He has died for us, bearing our sin and punishment to free us to live perfectly before God for all eternity. The world does not know that the cure for the cancer of sin is now available. They cannot know unless we tell them. We must share the good news—share it *regardless of circumstances*. We must always remember:

⇒ we are not the victims of circumstances; we are the conquerors of circumstances—all for Jesus Christ.
⇒ we are not to allow our circumstances to discourage others; we are to use our circumstances to encourage others.

b. *Paul spread the gospel by encouraging other believers* to be more fearless in witnessing. How was this possible? Note several things.
   ⇒ Paul's dynamic witness and the converts among the Imperial guard were being talked about all over the city. Of course, the new converts among the soldiers were beginning to share Christ.
   ⇒ Paul's fellow ministers who visited him (Timothy and others) were sharing news about Paul and witnessing themselves.
   ⇒ Paul was allowed visitors. While he was a prisoner, many of the believers throughout Rome visited him, and he boldly shared Christ with them. Note what is said:

   "And Paul dwelt two whole years in his own hired house, and received all that came in unto him, preaching the kingdom of God, and teaching those things which concern the Lord Jesus Christ, with all confidence, no man forbidding him" (Acts 28:30-31. Read the brief account for an encouraging picture of just how much Paul shared the gospel—no matter his circumstances, Acts 28:17-31.)

Paul's dynamic witness made a strong impact upon all those around him. His strong witness, despite his terrible circumstances, stirred *many* believers to become much more confident in their own witnessing—no matter their circumstances.

33

"And he said unto them, Go ye into all the world, and preach the gospel to every creature" (Mk.16:15).

APPLICATION:
Personal witnessing is simply finding out where a person is and moving him or her as far as possible toward a real relationship with the Lord Jesus. Witnessing is a natural outflow of God's working in our lives. Before tomorrow comes, ask God for a "chance" meeting with someone who would be open to your witness. Remember, it is God who does the saving. Our job is to simply share Christ everywhere we go.

2. A MATURE WITNESS HOLDS NO PERSONAL JEALOUSY NOR DESIRE FOR CREDIT OR PRESTIGE (v.15-18).

This is a strange experience shared by Paul, yet it is an experience that is so often and tragically repeated in the church and among believers. Some preachers in Rome were jealous of Paul and envious...
- of the results he was having.
- of the favorable attention and prestige he was gaining from society and the social circles of the community.
- of the support and loyalty believers were giving him.
- of the attention he was receiving from so many of their members.
- of the position he was gaining as the leader of the Christian community in Rome.

Note: the preachers were true followers of Christ. They were not the Judaizers, the false preachers who sometimes followed and opposed Paul. These were genuine preachers who were ministers in and around the metropolis of Rome. We know this because Paul agreed with their preaching; he just regretted their opposition to him. Instead of supporting him, they were speaking out against him, hoping to silence his influence and get rid of him (v.16).

However, not all the preachers throughout Rome opposed Paul. Some were preaching Christ out of love, and they were encouraging their members to show their love for Paul by visiting and supporting him in his ministry of proclaiming Christ.

APPLICATION:
How often has this scene been repeated? How many are repeating the scene right now? How many believers and Christian workers are jealous and envious...
- of the position of someone else?
- of the attention, support, and loyalty that someone else receives?
- of the results that another worker is having?

How many of us begin to question and speak against a servant of the Lord because of these things, speak quietly perhaps to only one or two others; nevertheless, we do speak out? God forgive us!

We must always remember: we are *all* ministers and workers if we have been truly saved by Christ. Each one has his call, and no matter the call, the road is always difficult. Therefore, we must support each other. The Lord does not require *big ministries* and *big names* and *big followers* from us all. What he requires is faithfulness—faithfulness in the ministry to which he has called us. Therefore, let us be *faithful* and support all the ministers of the gospel of Christ. As members of the church, of the same body of Christ, we need to put down our pride and learn to work together for the common cause—to spread the gospel of Jesus Christ.

> **"Peter seeing him saith to Jesus, Lord, and what shall this man do? Jesus saith unto him, If I will that he tarry till I come, what is that to thee? follow thou me" (Jn.21:21-22).**

QUESTIONS:
1. Have you ever done a job or good deed with a pure motive only to have someone accuse you of 'brown-nosing' or trying to win someone's favor?
2. How did you react?
3. How should you react?
4. How can we keep a pure heart in relation to someone else's ministry and achievements?

3. A MATURE WITNESS POSSESSES THE ASSURANCE OF A HAPPY ENDING: SALVATION (v.19).

Again, remember Paul's circumstances: he was in prison, but he was still preaching Christ. And because he was so faithful to his call—faithful in preaching Christ—God was honoring his preaching. Tremendous results were occurring: unbelievers from all over were being saved, and believers were being encouraged to step forward and become bolder witnesses for Christ. The result was that everyone throughout all of Rome, believers and non-believers, were talking about Paul, esteeming and holding him ever so highly in their minds. So much attention, support, and loyalty were being showered upon him that some of the local preachers were becoming nervous, jealous, and envious. The result: they began to speak out against Paul and his ministry.

The point of the present verse is this: Paul is sure God will save and deliver him from their criticism and opposition. He is sure of God's help and deliverance because of two things:

1. There was the prayer of those who supported him—both those in Rome and those around the world who were praying for him daily. Note that he was writing to the Philippians, so he knew they would begin to pray for him immediately, and God answered their prayers. Therefore, he knew that God would deliver him from such antagonistic opposition because the Philippians were praying for him even if no one else were. What a glorious teaching and goal for every church—to be so strong in the Lord that the answers to her prayers are always assured!

2. The Holy Spirit would deliver him. Paul knew that the Holy Spirit would supply whatever he needed to get through his circumstances. No matter what our need is nor how great our need is, the Holy Spirit will deliver us.

ILLUSTRATION:
A popular story is told about a man who was hiking on the edge of a very high cliff. In his haste to get to his destination, he slipped and found himself in a free-fall. Desperately, luckily, he was able to grab a branch of a tree that was growing out of the side of the cliff. Thankful that there was a tree there to save him from his sudden collision on the sharp rocks below, he quickly began to plot how to save himself.

His options were few: hang on to the branch with all his might; let go and finish his surely fatal free-fall; or hope that someone on top of the cliff could hear him. *"Hey! Is there anyone up there?!"* In response to his desperate cry, an unseen voice from above called out to him, *"Let go of the branch. I can help you then!"*

The hiker in peril spent little time meditating on the unseen voice's offer..."Is anybody else up there?!"

Unlike this hiker, when the Christian finds himself out on a limb for God, he can have the assurance of a happy ending: God will save him.

QUESTIONS:
1. Who or what do you have a tendency to turn to when things get tough? (Family, friends, worldly things, drugs, alcohol.)
2. When you get in a tight spot, what has God promised to do for you according to verse 19?
3. Who prayed for you to become a Christian believer? Did you know that they were praying for you? Who prays for you on a regular basis now?
4. What kind of relationship do you think the Holy Spirit wants to have with you? How can you develop that relationship?

SUMMARY:

God expects us to become mature witnesses for Him. God expects us to:
1. Share the gospel, regardless of circumstances
2. Hold no personal desire for credit or glory
3. Be assured of a happy ending, that of salvation

PERSONAL JOURNAL NOTES:
(Reflection & Response)

1. The most important thing that I learned from this lesson was:

2. The area that I need to work on the most is:

3. I can apply this lesson to my life by:

4. Closing Statement of Commitment:

---

[1]Dr. Bill Bright, *Witnessing Without Fear* (San Bernadino, CA: Here's Life Publishers, 1987), p.13-14.
[2]Rev. Mark Guy Pearse, Quoted in *Three Thousand Illustrations for Christian Service* by Walter B. Knight, p.69.

		I shall choose I wot not.	Christ
	D. The Marks of the Great Christian Believer, 1:20-26	23 For I am in a strait betwixt two, having a desire to depart, and to	
1. One great expectation & hope: To magnify Christ in his body	20 According to my earnest expectation and my hope, that in nothing I shall be ashamed, but that with all boldness, as always, so now also Christ shall be magnified in my body, whether it be by life, or by death.	be with Christ; which is far better: 24 Nevertheless to abide in the flesh is more needful for you. 25 And having this confidence, I know that I shall abide and continue with you all for your furtherance	**4. One great willingness: To serve sacrificially**
2. One great commitment in life & death: Christ	21 For to me to live is Christ, and to die is gain.	and joy of faith; 26 That your rejoicing may be more abundant	a. By proclaiming the believer's faith
3. One great dilemma: Whether To live or to depart to be with	22 But if I live in the flesh, this is the fruit of my labour: yet what	in Jesus Christ for me by my coming to you again.	b. By fellowshipping with believers

Section I
THE MARKS OF GOD'S PEOPLE, Philippians 1:1-30

Study 4: THE MARKS OF THE GREAT CHRISTIAN BELIEVER

Text: Philippians 1:20-26

Aim: To firmly adopt the marks of a great Christian believer.

Memory Verse:
> "For to me to live is Christ, and to die is gain" (Philippians 1:21).

INTRODUCTION:

There are two kinds of Christian believers: those who *MARVEL* & those who are *MARVELED AT*. Greatness comes to the Christian when he becomes committed to the cause of Christ.

Athletes become great when they make a total commitment to their sport. They fully understand the need to do what is best for their bodies. Their commitments become a matter of life and death. The committed athlete enjoys a challenge but is always pressing for even greater challenges. Greatness comes to an athlete who is willing to sacrifice everything.

It is easy to settle for a marginal life, but God has a better plan for His people: Greatness!

If a man has ever lived a life of commitment to our Lord Jesus Christ, it was Paul. Remember, he was in prison facing a capital crime with his deliverance looking almost hopeless. Death was staring him in the face. This passage is one of the great passages of Scripture. Verse 21 has been adopted by many believers as their life verse. Many have committed their lives to pursue either verse twenty or twenty-one. This is the personal testimony of Paul: the marks of the great Christian believer: a life of commitment.

OUTLINE:
1. There is one great expectation and hope: to magnify Christ in one's body (v.20).
2. There is one great commitment in life and death: Christ (v.21).
3. There is one great dilemma: whether to live or to depart to be with Christ (v.22-23).
4. There is one great willingness: to serve sacrificially (v.24-26).

1. ONE GREAT EXPECTATION & HOPE: TO MAGNIFY CHRIST IN ONE'S BODY (v.20).

1. Note the words "earnest expectation." The Greek means to gaze into the distance with the head erect and outstretched just like a watchman on a tower. It is aiming one's attention at an object with concentration, eagerness, and intensity. It is turning the eyes away from everything else to focus upon one object alone. It is total concentration upon a person's desire.

2. Note what Paul's expectation and hope was. Remember Paul was in prison being charged with a capital crime which carried with it the penalty of death. The one hope of most prisoners would be release from prison or to have the death penalty reduced to a lesser punishment. But note Paul's "earnest expectation and hope": to magnify Christ in his body. Paul's mind was not upon his terrible plight and circumstances; it was upon Christ. As a prisoner he wanted to guard his body from...

- wondering and questioning God
- becoming discouraged and depressed
- becoming complacent and lethargic
- becoming inactive and undisciplined
- denying and turning away from God
- reacting and cursing God

Paul knew the weakness of the human body, how it tended toward...

• doubt	• self-satisfaction	• enslavement
• questioning	• extravagance	• neglecting God
• self-centeredness	• laziness	• ignoring God
• pride		

Since his conversion, Paul had totally committed himself to magnifying Christ. And there was only one place where Christ could be *magnified and seen*: that was in his body.

3. Note the reference to "by life, or by death." Paul was facing death. He did not know if he was to die or continue living. If he were to be executed, he wanted to be as faithful as ever and to magnify Christ in death. If he were to be declared innocent and set free, he wanted to continue to magnify Christ in his body.

4. Note why Paul wanted Christ to be magnified in his body: that he might not be ashamed in anything. Paul knew that he was going to face the same thing that every believer is to face: the judgment seat of Christ. He knew that everyone of us has to give an account for what we have done with our bodies while on earth.

> "For we must all appear before the judgment seat of Christ; that every one may receive the things done in his body, according to that he hath done, whether it be good or bad" (2 Cor.5:10).

When believers face Christ in judgment, the experience will not necessarily be peaches and cream.

⇒ There will be some believers who will be ashamed.

> "And now, little children, abide in him; that when he shall appear, we may have confidence, and not be <u>ashamed</u> before him at his coming" (1 Jn.2:28).

⇒ There will be some believers who will suffer loss and look like a burned out building.

> **"Every man's work shall be made manifest: for the day shall de-clare it, because it shall be revealed by fire; and the fire shall try every man's work of what sort it is. If any man's work abide which he hath built thereupon, he shall receive a reward. If any man's work shall be burned, he shall suffer loss: but he himself shall be saved; yet so _as by fire_" (1 Cor.3:13-15).**

This is what Paul meant: he did not want to be ashamed when he stood before Christ. He loved Christ with all his heart, for Christ had done so much for him. Therefore, his one expectation and hope was for Christ to be magnified in his body. He wanted Christ to be honored both in his life and in his death. Above all, he did not want to be ashamed when he stood before his wonderful Lord.

> **"And he said to them all, If any man will come after me, let him deny himself, and take up his cross daily and follow me. For whoso-ever will save his life shall lose it: but whosoever will lose his life for my sake, the same shall save it" (Lk.9:23-24).**

QUESTIONS:
1. What are some things that we as Christian believers do in our bodies that bring shame to Christ?
2. Are there some things in your life that are bringing shame to Christ?
3. What are some very practical things you can do to magnify Christ in your body?

2. ONE GREAT COMMITMENT IN LIFE & DEATH: CHRIST (v.21).

Paul made two phenomenal statements:
1. He declared, "To me to live is Christ." What did he mean by this? He meant at least five things.
    a. He presented his body as a living sacrifice to Jesus Christ.

> **"I beseech you therefore, brethren, by the mercies of God, that ye present your bodies a living sacrifice, holy, acceptable unto God, which is your reasonable service" (Ro.12:1).**

    b. He struggled to yield every part of his body to Christ as a tool for righteousness.

> **"Neither yield ye your members [bodily parts] as instruments of unrighteousness unto sin: but yield yourselves unto God, as those that are alive from the dead, and your members as instruments of righteousness unto God" (Ro.6:13).**

    c. He struggled to control his mind—to control every thought and to focus every thought upon Jesus Christ and the great virtues of life.

> **"Casting down imaginations, and every high thing that exalteth itself against the knowledge of God, and bringing into captivity every thought to the obedience of Christ" (2 Cor.10:5).**

> **"Whatsoever things are true, whatsoever things are honest, whatsoever things are just, whatsoever things are pure, whatsoever things are lovely, whatsoever things are of good report; if**

there be any virtue, and if there be any praise, think on these things" (Ph.4:8).

d. He committed himself to work for love and justice within all of society.

> "Therefore all things whatsoever ye would that men should do to you, do ye even so to them: for this is the law and the prophets" (Mt.7:12).

e. He gave his life—every moment of it—to reach and minister to as many people as possible during his journey upon earth.

> "Then said Jesus to them again, Peace be unto you: as my Father hath sent me, even so send I you" (Jn.20:21).

2. He declared that "to die is gain." He knew better than to base his life upon the worldly pleasures and possessions of this earth. He knew that everything upon earth was aging and passing away including man himself. Therefore, Paul reached out for a Savior, a Person who could save him and give him an eternal world that would never age or pass away. This is the reason he grabbed hold of Christ. Jesus Christ is God's only begotten Son sent into the world to reveal the truth of another world to us, a world that is permanent and that has no corruption—no aging—no passing away in it. Therefore, Paul grabbed hold of Christ when he found out...

*   that Christ saved men from sin, death, and condemnation.
*   that Christ made it possible for men to live forever with God in a new heaven and earth.

> "For God so loved the world, that he gave his only begotten Son, that whosoever believeth in him should not perish, but have everlasting life" (Jn.3:16).

QUESTIONS:
What are you living for? What is your great purpose in life?
⇒ Are you living for money and possessions (clothes, houses, cars, property)? If so, what happens when you die? When that day comes—and it is coming—what good will your money and possessions do you?
⇒ Are you living for comfort (a good job, a nice place to live, plenty to eat, and enough money to do what you desire now and at retirement)? If so, what happens when disease or accident or tragedy strikes or old age comes? And one or the other is coming. It cannot be stopped. If you have lived for comfort, what good will it do you?
⇒ Are you living for a position? If so, what do you do when you are edged out, removed, demoted, transferred, by-passed, faced with disease or accident? What good will position do you?
⇒ Are you living for family? If so, what do you do when the family has transferred, moved away, or various family members die? And it happens to everyone of us. What good will family do you when you face Christ?
⇒ Are you living for recognition, honor, popularity, recreation, gratification, sensuality—whatever? What do you do when you face the crises of life and then in the end come face to face with death? At that moment if not before, what good will anything on this earth do you?

3. ONE GREAT DILEMMA: WHETHER TO LIVE OR TO DEPART TO BE WITH CHRIST (v.22,23).
The great Christian believer has one great dilemma—whether to live or to depart and be with Christ. The word "depart" is descriptive. It has a twofold meaning that speaks to the believer's heart.

1.   It means to break up; to loosen as in breaking camp and loosening the ropes of the tent. It is the picture of packing up and moving on to a new location. The same picture is true of the believer when he *departs* this life. He is not ceasing to exist; he is simply breaking loose and moving on to a new campsite, in fact, a perfect campsite.

2.   It means to loosen the moorings of a ship, weigh anchor, and set sail for another port. Again, the believer does not cease to exist, he simply loosens the moorings of this life, pulls the anchor up, and sets sail for God's eternal presence.

Paul says that he is caught between two great desires:

⇒ One desire is to live a life of fruitful service for the Lord Jesus Christ.

⇒ The other desire is to depart and go on to be with Christ which is far better.

The natural mind wonders and questions how a person in his right mind could ever want to go ahead and die. The reason is simply answered: the genuine believer does not die; he never tastes death. When it is time for him to leave this earth, he is immediately transferred into the presence of Christ. Immediately—quicker than the blinking of an eye—the believer is transported into the perfect world of God which is named heaven. The believer is perfected—never again to experience pain, suffering, sin, corruption, infirmity, weakness, deformity, disappointment, fear, loss, or death. He will be perfected to work for Christ throughout the new heavens and earth, and he will serve and worship Christ for ever and ever. The promises of God to the believer are phenomenal; they just explode the human mind. It is for this reason that the believer can declare: "To die is gain."

⇒ There is the promise of never dying.

> **"[God's grace] is now made manifest by the appearing of our Saviour Jesus Christ, who hath abolished death, and hath brought life and immortality to light through the gospel" (2 Tim.1:10).**

⇒ There is the promise of being with the Lord Jesus Christ Himself forever and ever.

> **"In my Father's house are many mansions: if it were not so, I would have told you. I go to prepare a place for you. And if I go and prepare a place for you, I will come again, and receive you unto myself; that where I am, there ye may be also" (Jn.14:2-3).**

⇒ There is the promise of receiving a glorious body just like our Lord's glorious body.

> **"Now this I say, brethren, that flesh and blood cannot inherit the kingdom of God; neither doth corruption inherit incorruption. Behold, I show you a mystery; We shall not all sleep, but we shall all be changed, in a moment, in the twinkling of an eye, at the last trump: for the trumpet shall sound, and the dead shall be raised incorruptible, and we shall be changed. For this corruptible must put on incorruption, and this mortal must put on immortality" (1 Cor.15:50-53).**

⇒ There is the promise of being made an heir of God.

> **"The Spirit itself beareth witness with our spirit, that we are the children of God: and if children, then heirs; heirs of God, and jointheirs with Christ; if so be that we suffer with him, that we may be also glorified together" (Ro.8:16-17).**

⇒ There is the promise of ruling and reigning with Christ forever and ever.

> **"His lord said unto him, Well done, good and faithful servant; thou hast been faithful over a few things, I will make thee ruler over many things: enter thou into the joy of thy lord" (Mt.25:23).**

PHILIPPIANS 1:20-26

The faithful believer sometimes aches to go on to be with the Lord. It will be a wonderful day of *union* with our Lord and a glorious day of reunion with all our loved ones who have gone on before us. The only word that can adequately express all that God has prepared for us who know Him is the word that is the same in all human languages: *Hallelujah!*

> **"Therefore be ye also ready: for in such an hour as ye think not**
> **the Son of man cometh" (Mt.24:44).**

ILLUSTRATION:

How strong is your perception of eternity?

We live in a day and time where medical technology has taken great strides by keeping people alive who would have died years ago. There are both positive and negative points for the Christian believer to consider.

For example, look at the life of a young lady whom we will call Karen. At the prime of her life, Karen was stricken by a devastating disease which put her in a coma. Years went by as she lay asleep. The only thing that was keeping her alive was a series of tubes which had become new appendages to her body.

Karen's parents finally made the difficult decision to turn off the life-support machines and remove the tubes from their daughter's wasted body. Their decision was not easy. It was so hard to let her go. But it was bearable because of Karen's commitment to Christ. When she finally left this world, she fell into the arms of her loving heavenly Father.

When you let go of this old world, will you fall into His arms also?

APPLICATION:

Many have gone before us. Those who are in Christ will have a glorious eternity to spend together.

Tragically, those who never give their hearts to Jesus will be eternally separated from God (and from the saints in Christ). This should be a burden that compels the believer to pray for the lost and share the gospel with them.

QUESTIONS:

1. Are you ready to die and to leave this world? Are you confident of where you will spend eternity?
2. What are the things of this world that are the hardest to think of giving up?
3. For now, God has permitted you to remain in this world for a reason. What would that reason(s) be?
4. Who do you have a burden for that would miss Heaven if they died today? What kinds of things can you do to reach out and witness to them.

4. ONE GREAT WILLINGNESS: TO SERVE SACRIFICIALLY (v.24-26).

Sitting there in prison waiting for the trial that would determine whether he lived or died, something happened to Paul. Either through thinking about the needs that existed in the world and in the churches, or through some sense from the Holy Spirit, Paul became convinced that he would be found innocent of the false charges and released from prison. But note why: it was not for his sake and enjoyment of life but so that he could continue to minister.

The point to see is Paul's heart—how it longed to reach people for Christ and to meet the needs of a world that reels under the weight of desperation.

> **"Let us therefore follow after the things which make for peace, and**
> **things wherewith one may edify another" (Ro.14:19).**

PHILIPPIANS 1:20-26

ILLUSTRATION:

What kinds of thoughts enter the heart of a Christian believer who willingly serves Christ? Here is one example:

"Dwight L. Moody was the Billy Graham of the nineteenth century. On his first trip to England a young Moody heard these challenging words which would radically alter his life:

"The world has yet to see what God will do with, and for, and through, and in, and by, the man who is fully and wholly consecrated to Him.

"He said 'a man,' thought Moody; he did not say a great man, nor a learned man, nor a rich man, nor a wise man, nor an eloquent man, nor a smart man, but simply a man. I am a man, and it lies with the man himself whether he will, or will not, make that entire and full consecration. I will try my utmost to be that man."[1]

QUESTIONS:

1. What things tend to get in the way of your service and sacrifice to the Lord?
2. What has to change in you for there to be a desire to serve and sacrifice?
3. What are some things that you need to sacrifice in order to fully serve the Lord and His people?
4. Are you at a place in your life to make the same commitment that Moody made to God? Why or why not?

SUMMARY:

God has called every believer to be a great Christian. God wants us all to have...
1. One great expectation and hope: to magnify Christ in our bodies.
2. One great commitment in life and death: Christ.
3. One great dilemma: whether to live or to depart to be with Christ.
4. One great willingness: to serve sacrificially.

PERSONAL JOURNAL NOTES:
(Reflection & Response)

1. The most important thing that I learned from this lesson was:

2. The area that I need to work on the most is:

3. I can apply this lesson to my life by:

4. Closing Statement Of Commitment:

---

[1] Pat Morley, *The Rest Of Your Life* (Nashville, TN: Thomas Nelson, 1992), p.237-238.

43

	E. The Marks of the Great Christian Church, 1:27-30	28 And in nothing terrified by your adversaries: which is to them an evident token of perdition, but to you of salvation, and that of God.	4. Mark 4: Courage & fearlessness
1. Mark 1: Christian conduct—heavenly citizenship	27 Only let your conversation be as it becometh the gospel of Christ: that whether I come and see you, or		a. Persecution is a sign of destruction
2. Mark 2: Honoring the gospel			b. Persecution is a sign of salvation
3. Mark 3: Standing fast	else be absent, I may hear of your affairs,	29 For unto you it is given in the behalf of Christ, not only to believe on him, but also to suffer for his sake;	c. Persecution is a privilege
a. Must stand fast in one spirit & with one mind	that ye stand fast in one spirit, with one mind striving together		
b. Must stand fast in striving together for the faith of the gospel	for the faith of the gospel.	30 Having the same conflict which ye saw in me, and now hear to be in me.	d. Paul left a dynamic example in bearing persecution

Section I
THE MARKS OF GOD'S PEOPLE, Philippians 1:1-30

Study 5:   THE MARKS OF THE GREAT CHRISTIAN CHURCH

Text: Philippians 1:27-30

Aim: To make a serious commitment to build a great Christian church.

Memory Verse:
"For unto you it is given in the behalf of Christ, not only to believe on Him, but also to suffer for His sake" (Philippians 1:29).

INTRODUCTION:
Think for a moment. What is the *mission* of the church? The *mission* of the church is the "Great Com*mission*." Any church that is structured with the Great Commission in mind will become a Great Church.

Listen to this brief quote:

"We have structured too many churches for the sake and comfort of those who already are Christians and are attending them, rather than for the sake of those people who are un-churched....Church members without question assume that the church exists to meet their needs, and they therefore structure their programs and build their facility with that in mind"[1]

Do you think this is true? Are we missing the mark in our churches? What makes a Christian church great?
⇒ A large physical building?
⇒ Hi-tech programs for every age group?
⇒ A leader with a charismatic personality?

The apostle Paul did not mention any of this in his letter to the church at Philippi. His approach took on a completely different tone. Paul was in prison. He faced a capital crime, and there was a strong chance he might be executed. He did not think so, but there was a possibility. He was not sure if he would ever see the Philippian church again, so he sat down and began to write to them. What would you say if you were writing to a group of God's people for the last time? One of the subjects that concerned Paul was the subject of this passage: the marks of a great church. The Philippian church was a great church, and Paul wanted it to remain great. Therefore, he reviewed with them the marks of a great Christian church.

OUTLINE:
1. Mark 1: Christian conduct—heavenly citizenship (v.27).
2. Mark 2: honoring the gospel (v.27).
3. Mark 3: standing fast (v.27).
4. Mark 4: courage and fearlessness (v.28-30).

1. MARK 1: CHRISTIAN CONDUCT—HEAVENLY CITIZENSHIP (v.27).

The *conversation* or *conduct* of a church is significant. Paul was writing to the church at Philippi about their conduct. Philippi was a proud Roman colony. In fact, it was famous as a miniature Rome. A city became a Roman colony in one of two ways. At first Rome founded colonies throughout the outer reaches of the Empire to keep the peace and to guard against invasions from barbaric hordes. Veteran soldiers, ready for retirement, were usually granted citizenship if they would go out and settle these colonies. Later on, however, a city was granted the distinctive title of a Roman Colony for loyalty and service to the Empire. The distinctive thing about these colonies was their fanatic loyalty to Rome. The citizens kept all their Roman ties: the Roman language, titles, customs, affairs, and dress. They refused to allow any infiltration of local influence whatsoever. They totally rejected the influence of the world around them. They were Roman colonists within an alien environment.

The Philippian church knew exactly what Paul was saying: they were citizens of heaven. Therefore, they must...
- keep their close ties with heaven.
- speak the clean and pure language of heaven.
- bear the title of heaven, Christian, and do so proudly.
- bear witness to the customs of heaven.
- carry on the affairs of heaven.
- dress as a citizen of heaven.
- allow no infiltration of worldly influence whatsoever.
- live and conduct themselves as a heavenly colony within a polluted and dying environment.

> **"And this I pray, that your love may abound yet more and more in knowledge and in all judgment; that ye may approve things that are excellent; that ye may be sincere and without offence till the day of Christ" (Ph.1:9-10).**

ILLUSTRATION:
Have you ever travelled to another country? For those who have, they understand the need for a passport. If you travel abroad, one of your most valuable possessions is your passport. Your passport validates your citizenship, permits you to travel across international borders, grants you all the rights as a citizen of your *home country*—if you should ever need help from your embassy or consulate. Your passport has another important feature: it allows you to come home.

So it is with our 'heavenly passport.' Being sealed by the Holy Spirit is for us, a precious possession. His work in our heart validates the fact that our citizenship is in Heaven. We are just passing through this world: in it, but not of it.

Because we belong to Him, He has given us His Kingdom and all of its rights. When we need help in this world, He invites us to call upon Him for help. Finally, having a heavenly passport grants us immediate access to the Father—whenever we need Him (which is all day long). And when He calls us home for good, forever, our heavenly passport (the redemptive work of His Son) will allow us to walk through Heaven's gates with a song of rejoicing!

1. Do you truly *think* of earth as your temporary home?
2. Do you *live* like earth is your temporary home? Or do you get caught up in the affairs of this world and its material traps?
3. How can you go about your daily life and identify with a heavenly home? Is it realistic?
4. Do you need to make any adjustments in order to be a better citizen of heaven?

2. MARK 2: HONORING THE GOSPEL (v.27).

The word "becometh" means to fit, to be suitable, to be worthy. The believer's behavior is to...
- fit the gospel he professes.
- be suitable to the gospel he professes.
- be worthy of the gospel he professes.

No church and no believer within the church is to bring dishonor to the gospel. If a person professes the gospel he is to live worthy of the gospel.

We can compare it to a piece of clothing that is attractive upon a person, that is becoming to a person. What we mean is that the clothing matches and enhances the person's looks and personality. The same is true with the gospel of Christ. If we put on the gospel, we are to wear the gospel. Scripture declares:

"Adorn the doctrine of God our Savior in all things" (Tit.2:10).

QUESTIONS:
1. What conclusions do you make when someone does not dress appropriately?
2. How would the people who know you best judge your "gospel wardrobe"?
   a)   On the best-dressed list—you wear the gospel well and enhance it.
   b)   Sharp-looking threads, but a little over-done—you're trying a little too hard to act like you're 'wearing the gospel.'
   c)   About 20 years behind the current fashions—you're not in tune with what's happening in the world, so your efforts are useless!
   d)   Nothing matches—you don't even care about what you wear or how you appear to others. You do your own thing.
   e)   Your clothes do not fit—you're trying to wear something that doesn't really suit you.
   f)   More holes than hems—you occasionally 'put on' the gospel, but usually you don't bother.
   g)   A spiritual streaker: nothing on at all—there is no evidence of the gospel in your life.
3. How can you become more worthy and suitable to "wear" the gospel? What kinds of things can you do to change?

3. MARK 3: STANDING FAST (v.27).

Remember that Paul was in prison, awaiting trial on a capital charge. There was a chance he would be executed for a false crime. He thought he would be released, but he was not absolutely sure. Therefore, whether he was able to return to the church or not, there was a much needed exhortation that the church must heed: the exhortation to stand fast.
   1.   The church must stand fast in *unity*: "in one spirit, with one mind."
        ⇒   *One spirit* means that all the members of a church must be born again by the Spirit of Christ. All members must have a renewed spirit from the same source, from the same Person. They must all be committed to the Lord Jesus Christ. They must all have a heart given to Him.
        ⇒   *One mind* means that all members must be set upon the same purpose; they must all be focused upon the purpose of Jesus Christ.

The point is this: the world—its people, families, and nations—may be split and divided, arguing and differing, fussing and feuding, fighting and divorcing, warring and killing, seeking and grasping; but the church is not to live that way. The church is to be unified; it is to be one in spirit and one in mind; one in heart and one in purpose.

> "Now I beseech you, brethren, by the name of our Lord Jesus Christ, that ye all speak the same thing, and that there be no divisions among you; but that ye be perfectly joined together in the same mind and in the same judgment" (1 Cor.1:10).

2. The church must stand fast in striving together for the faith of the gospel. The word "striving together" is the word taken from an athletic contest. It is the picture of a team working and struggling together against strong opposition (cp. a football team). The church—every member of it—is to strive for the faith of the gospel: strive, work, struggle, push, exert all the energy possible; everyone cooperating together, not a single person letting up or turning aside or walking off the field. The opposition is difficult; therefore, the faith of the gospel needs every member working and struggling together.

> "Therefore, my beloved brethren, be ye stedfast, unmoveable, always abounding in the work of the Lord, forasmuch as ye know that your labour is not in vain in the Lord" (1 Cor.15:58).

QUESTIONS:
1. How would you describe your church in terms of "striving together":
   a) A great team-effort: everyone contributes
   b) Kind of sluggish: a lack of energy
   c) No team-work: everyone does his own thing
   d) Lots of grandstanding: individual people looking for glory
2. What part do you play on the church team? Can you make a difference? What things can you do to make a difference?

4. MARK 4: COURAGE AND FEARLESSNESS (v.28-30).

Being a Christian believer in a corrupt world is hard. People oppose our stand for Christ and righteousness. It may be next door, in the office, at school or a hundred other places—the Christian believer is sometimes...

• avoided	• ignored	• cursed	• slandered
• ridiculed	• neglected	• questioned	• persecuted
• mocked	• overlooked	• abused	• imprisoned
• isolated	• by-passed	• mistreated	• martyred

Note the exhortation: we are not to be terrified by our adversaries. There are four reasons why.
1. *Persecution is a sign that the persecutors are doomed.* And note: it is a sign *to them*. The Spirit of God is able to take their persecution of us and convict their hearts of the evil they are doing. Their persecution of a fellow human being strikes the fact of doom and judgment to their hearts: it convicts them, and by that conviction they stand a better chance of being saved.
2. *Persecution is a sign of salvation for us.* Of course, it is not the only sign, but it is one sign. If a believer stands fast in persecution, it is a clear sign that he is being strengthened by the Spirit of God and is a true believer.
3. *Persecution is a privilege, not a terror.* When we are persecuted, we are suffering for Christ, the Sovereign Majesty of the universe. Christ is not some *insignificant rebel*, some *leader of men* hiding out in some remote spot who embarrasses us and of whom we should be ashamed. Christ is the Son of God, the Lord of lords, the God of the universe, the Sovereign Majesty of all. It is a privilege to be numbered among His followers and to represent Him. If we happen to be cornered by some who oppose and rebel against Him, we are not to deny Him nor

be ashamed to own His name. We are not to be terrified by persecution. It is the highest honor imaginable to represent and serve the Lord God of all. He is coming soon to subject all opponents and enemies, ruling and reigning over all. We could have no greater privilege than preparing the way for Him—even if some do oppose us.

4.   *Paul (and others) had left the church a dynamic example to follow in bearing persecution.* Paul had been arrested, beaten, and jailed when he was in Philippi; and the church had witnessed the whole scene. He bore it all for Christ. Therefore, we are to follow in his steps and bear whatever persecution is launched against us—all for Christ. The great Christian soldier can bear it through the presence and power of Christ.

ILLUSTRATION:

The story is told of a Chinese Christian who lived during the early years when the communists came to power. After being offered his life in exchange for renouncing his faith in Christ, he was finally placed before a firing squad. After the blind-fold was in place, the piercing chant from the regiment's officer rang in everyone's ears: "Ready...Aim...Fire," and suddenly this Chinese Christian found himself in the eternal arms of his Savior.

Trusting in Christ will carry the believer from this world to the next.

"**Remember the word that I said unto you, The servant is not greater than his lord. If they have persecuted me, they will also persecute you; if they have kept my saying, they will keep yours also**" (Jn.15:20).

QUESTIONS:

1. What are some ways you are persecuted in this day and age? Who persecutes you?
2. What feelings rise up inside your heart when your are being persecuted for the sake of the gospel?
3. History has an outstanding record of displaying God's power when His church is persecuted. The apostle Paul is only one of many examples of a persecutor whose heart was turned to the Lord.
   Now, who is your "chief persecutor," the person who gives you the hardest time about your faith? What can you do or what has to be done to reach that person for Christ? (Be sure to pray that God will turn his or her heart—just like He did with Paul.)

SUMMARY:

A Church is great when it is structured like a Great Commission Church. When that is true, the following four marks are evident:
Mark 1: Christian conduct—heavenly citizenship
Mark 2: Honoring the gospel
Mark 3: Standing fast
Mark 4: Courage & fearlessness

PHILIPPIANS 1:27-30

PERSONAL JOURNAL NOTES:
(Reflection & Response)

1. The most important thing that I have learned from this lesson was:

2. The area that I need to work on the most is:

3. I can apply this lesson to my life by:

4. Closing Statement Of Commitment:

---

[1]Robert Logan, *Beyond Church Growth* (Grand Rapids, MI: Fleming H. Revell, 1989), p.63.

PHILIPPIANS 2:1-4

	CHAPTER 2 II. THE STEPS TO UNITY, 2:1-18 A. Christ--The Traits of His Life in Us, 2:1-4	2 Fulfil ye my joy, that ye be likeminded, having the same love, being of one accord, of one mind. 3 Let nothing be done through strife or vainglory; but in lowliness of mind let each es-	5. The trait of concern for one another's joy 6. The trait of humility or lowliness of mind
1. The trait of consolation 2. The trait of love 3. The trait of fellowship in the Spirit 4. The trait of compassion	If there be therefore any consolation in Christ, if any comfort of love, if any fellowship of the Spirit, if any bowels and mercies	teem other better than themselves. 4 Look not every man on his own things, but every man also on the things of others.	7. The trait of controlling self-interest or concentration upon oneself

Section II
THE STEPS TO UNITY, Philippians 2:1-18

Study 1:   CHRIST—THE TRAITS OF HIS LIFE IN US

Text: Philippians 2:1-4

Aim: To embrace the character traits of Christ: To become more like Him.

Memory Verse:
"Let nothing be done through strife or vainglory; but in lowliness of mind let each esteem other better than themselves" (Philippians 2:3).

INTRODUCTION:
In the classic novel by Charles Sheldon, "In His Steps," the community is challenged to live their lives just as if Jesus was living with them.

The attitudes of the people were dramatically changed as each one began to filter his thoughts and actions through this challenge. Needless to say, people began to change. Love and unity became the norm: just because they were walking in His steps.

What a challenge for us as well! Jesus has promised to be with us and to offer us the privilege of walking in His steps. As each of us know, saying we will do it is a whole lot easier than actually doing His will.

The Philippian church was a very strong church. When a church is strong, it is always full of vision and planning, and it is always working out a strategy to carry forth the gospel. A strong church launches ministry after ministry and program after program. It is never still and never complacent—neither the minds of the people nor the hands of the people. Because of this, there is always the danger of differences of opinion: differences in vision, desires, concern, emphasis, and interest. There are always different ideas as to which ministry or project should be undertaken and supported and a host of other differences.

The point is this: the more strength and activity a church has, the more attention it must give to unity. Why? Because a strong church has more minds and bodies working, and where more people are working more differences are bound to arise. Consequently, the members must give more attention to unity.

PHILIPPIANS 2:1-4

Paul knew this; he knew that he had to put the Philippian church on guard. The church had to protect itself against disunity and division. This is the subject of chapter two: The Steps to Unity (2:1-18).

The first step to unity is Christ—allowing His life to be lived out in us. In particular there are seven traits that will hold the church together and keep it unified.

OUTLINE:
1. The trait of consolation (v.1).
2. The trait of love (v.1).
3. The trait of fellowship in the Spirit (v.1).
4. The trait of compassion (v.1).
5. The trait of concern for one another's joy (v.2).
6. The trait of humility or lowliness of mind (v.3).
7. The trait of controlling self-interest or concentration upon oneself (v.4).

1. THE TRAIT OF CONSOLATION (v.1).

Consolation means many things throughout Scripture; but in the present context it means encouragement, comfort, solace, and strengthening. Note that this trait is a characteristic of Christ Himself. The very beat of His Spirit is to encourage, comfort, and strengthen believers to be one in spirit and busy about the ministry of His church. Christ wants no murmuring, grumbling, disturbance, or weakening of the unity within the church. The Spirit of Christ is to take the disturbed or upset person and...

- console him.
- comfort him.
- encourage him.
- strengthen him.

Now glance at the charge of verse two:
⇒ "Be likeminded"—just like Christ: console, comfort, encourage, exhort, and strengthen each other.

Let absolutely nothing interfere with the spirit of unity in the church. But note, we are not only to help those who are disturbed, we are to let the comfort and encouragement of Christ flow in us when we are disturbed. When disturbed, we are to let Christ comfort us; and when others are disturbed, we are to comfort them. Just imagine the spirit of unity that would flow through a church if all the members would let the consolation of Christ flow through them. There would be no murmuring, grumbling, disturbance—no disunity whatsoever.

"I will not leave you comfortless: I will come to you" (Jn.14:18).

ILLUSTRATION:
Is encouragement a part of your daily agenda? "My Favorite Martian" was a popular old television program that featured an unusual fellow who could sense incoming signals around him. You see, he was equipped with a set of antenna.

God has equipped His people with a similar device: spiritual antenna that can pick up the signals from the Lord that direct us to other Christians who need encouragement.

What a miracle it is that we often receive a signal, a prompting from the Lord, that burdens us to encourage and minister...

- to the sick and dying
- to the poor and needy
- to the broken-hearted and back-slidden
- to the unsaved and lost
- to the lonely and empty
- to the orphan and widow

QUESTIONS:
1. Name some things that happen throughout life that cause people to need encouragement. How can you encourage them?
2. When a person in the church is being divisive, what can you do to calm, comfort, console, and help him?
3. Most likely you will meet someone this week who will need encouragement. Will you do it? How will it make you feel? The other person?

2. THE TRAIT OF LOVE (v.1).

There is a comfort of love that is in Christ. The love of Christ stirs a person to keep the unity with other believers. The word "love" is *agape love*, the love that is selfless and sacrificial. *Agape love* is the love of the mind, of the reason, and of the will. It is the love that goes so far...
- that it loves a person even if he does not deserve to be loved.
- that it actually loves the person who is utterly unworthy of being loved.

Agape love is the love of Christ, the love which He showed when He gave and sacrificed Himself for us. We did not deserve it and were utterly unworthy of such love, yet Christ loved us despite all.

Imagine the spirit of unity that would exist within a church if every member would let the love of Christ flow through him. There would be no bitterness, anger, or strife—no action that would hurt another person whatsoever. If the person was wrong and deserved punishment, the church's members would sacrifice and give themselves for him.

APPLICATION:
Note verse two:
⇒ **"Have the same love"**—the same love Christ had for you.

This is the answer to unity: the Lord's spirit of love! How desperately the church needs its members to let the love of Christ flow through them to each other! When someone hurts us the natural thing to do is strike back. The supernatural thing to do is to invite God's love into the situation. If you try His love, you will find no end to His resources to heal hurting people. What have you got to lose?

> **"A new commandment I give unto you, That ye love one another; as I have loved you, that ye also love one another. By this shall all men know that ye are my disciples, if ye have love one to another" (Jn.13:34-35).**

QUESTIONS:
1. What kinds of things make it hard for you to love people?
2. Is there anyone in your church whom you need to ask for forgiveness?
3. Is there someone you need to forgive?
4. Are there feelings of bitterness and strife that need to be confessed to the Lord?

3. THE TRAIT OF FELLOWSHIP IN THE SPIRIT (v.1).

Once a person has trusted Jesus Christ as his Lord, God's Spirit does two significant things to him.
⇒ *The Holy Spirit enters the believer's heart and life* to comfort, guide, teach, equip, and use him as a witness for Christ.
⇒ *The Holy Spirit creates a spiritual union* between the new believer and other believers. He melts and moulds the heart of the believer to the hearts of other believers. He attaches all their lives together, and they become one in life and purpose. They have a joint life sharing their blessings and needs and gifts together—all focused upon their Lord and His purpose.

The mind of the Holy Spirt is set upon unity and fellowship—all centered around Jesus Christ and His mission. The church and its believers are to have the same mind. There are to be no discordant elements whatsoever in the church: no talk about differences; no sharing of bad news; no gossip, rumors, cliques, nothing whatsoever that would tamper with or disturb the fellowship of the Spirit in the church. Again, quickly glance at verse two:

⇒ **"Be of one accord"**—keep the unity of the Spirit, the fellowship of the Spirit.

QUESTIONS:
1. Can you see the Holy Spirit? Do you feel the Holy Spirit in your life?
2. Do you find yourself forgetting that the Holy Spirit lives inside you?
3. Do you have a spiritual union with other Christians? How can this be explained?
4. What part did fellowship play in drawing you to your local church?

4. THE TRAIT OF COMPASSION (v.1).

Compassion is the trait that stirred Christ to reach out for us. Compassion is the force that drives Him to keep after us time and again—even if we are in rebellion and stand opposed to Him. We may be cantankerous; we may even curse Him and take up arms against His movement. But His compassion drives Him to stay after us so long as we live.

If we allowed His compassion to flow through us, can you not see what would happen in the church? What would happen if we were driven by compassion to go after those...
- who have been hurt?
- who differed?
- who withdrew?
- who have been disturbed?
- who were critical?

The list could go on and on. But just think how many would have already been reconciled back into the fellowship of the church if we had been compassionate and gone after them. Just think how much less trouble would have happened if we had reached out in *compassion* when a difference first appeared.

The point is this: we are to let the compassion of Christ flow both in and through us. His compassion will comfort us when we differ and are disturbed; it will stir us to reach out in compassion when others differ and become disturbed.The compassion of Jesus Christ flowing in and through us keeps the unity of the church. It will also keep our minds together—keep them focused upon the needs of a world that must be reached and ministered to in compassion.

> **"We then that are strong ought to bear the infirmities of the weak, and not to please ourselves" (Ro.15:1).**
> **"Bear ye one another's burdens, and so fulfil the law of Christ" (Gal.6:2).**

ILLUSTRATION:
It has been said that the church is not a club for saints but a hospital for sinners who have been wounded by the scars of sin.

Look around at the people you go to church with every week. Chances are that from outer appearances, all is well: the forced smile has been pasted on that morning; the deep pain of life has been pushed down into the depths of the heart; and the convenient cliche (I'm fine! How are you? Fine? That's fine...) comes to mind.

A church that has unity is that way because they have compassion for people. They have made a decision to become real and vulnerable. They have discovered by their own experience that the church should be a place for compassion. It is not a place for pretending.

5. THE TRAIT OF CONCERN FOR ONE ANOTHER'S JOY (v.2).

There is the trait of joy. The believers in a church are to be concerned for each other's joy. And note: the one thing that brings joy to a church quicker than anything else is unity.

"Fulfil ye my joy, that ye be likeminded, having the same love, being of one accord, of one mind" (v.2).

Paul's point is simple but direct: his joy in Christ would be fulfilled by only one thing—the unity of the Philippian church. The leaders and members of a church usually have joy in Christ, but their joy can be fulfilled only if unity exists between them. Joy is always disturbed when there is criticism, dissatisfaction, grumbling, murmuring, cliques, opposition, and a host of other divisive negatives. We are to worship, plan, organize, program, build, staff, finance, minister, and serve in the joy of Christ. But the only way we can do that is...

- to be likeminded.
- to have the same love.
- to be of one accord.
- to be of one mind.

"These things have I spoken unto you, that my joy might remain in you, and that your joy might be full" (Jn.15:11).

ILLUSTRATION:
Do your words fill others with joy? Listen to what Gary Smalley & John Trent have to say to us:

"Spoken words of blessing are so vital. They fortify relationships. They nurture and bolster self-esteem. They stimulate growth. And sometimes they can keep a worn-out traveler from stumbling on the road of life...A few carefully chosen words of comfort, encouragement, empathy, or insight—perhaps accompanied by a hug—can make all the difference between stumbling and moving on."[1]

6. THE TRAIT OF HUMILITY OR LOWLINESS OF MIND (v.3).

Note two significant points.
1. A strong and active church will always have two problems to stick their ugly heads up: *strife* and *empty glory*.

a. Some people are just going to *strive* with others. They are not mature in the Lord, not yet; therefore, they give in to...
- jealousy
- opposition
- forming cliques
- desire for recog- nition
- desire for position
- talking about dif- ferences
- loving flattery

If they do not get their way or what they want, they strive against the church or other members. The result is disunity and divisiveness, one of the most terrible crimes within the church to God.

"**Let nothing be done through strife or vainglory; but in lowliness of mind let each esteem other better than themselves**" (Ph.2:3).

b. Some people are going to *seek glory* within the church. But note what Scripture calls it: vainglory, which means empty glory. Some people just want the attention, the recognition, the position, the flattery, the praise, the honor. They want people seeking their advice and counsel and opinion. They want to be on the major committees and acknowledged as a leader of the church.

"**And whosoever shall exalt himself shall be abased; and he that shall humble himself shall be exalted**" (Mt.23:12).

2. The spirit that must prevail in a strong church is that of humility or lowliness of mind. In fact, the only way a church can remain strong and be blessed by God is for its people to walk in a spirit of humility.

A CLOSER LOOK:

Humility—Lowliness of Mind: *to offer* oneself as lowly and submissive; to walk in a spirit of lowliness; *to present* oneself as lowly and low-lying in mind; to be of low degree and low rank; not to be highminded, proud, haughty, arrogant, or assertive.

Note: a humble person may have a high position, power, wealth, fame, and much more; but he carries himself in a spirit of lowliness and submission. He denies himself for the sake of Christ and in order to help others.

Men have always looked upon humility as a vice. A lowly man is often looked upon as a coward, a cringing, despicable, slavish type of person. Men fear humility. They feel humility is a sign of weakness and will make them the object of contempt and abuse and cause them to be shunned and overlooked.

Because of all this, men ignore and shun the teaching of Christ on humility. This is tragic:
- ⇒ for a humble spirit is necessary for salvation (Mt.18:3-4).
- ⇒ for God's idea of humility is not weakness and cowardice.

God makes people strong, the strongest they can possibly be. By humility God does not mean what men mean. God infuses a new and strong spirit within a person and causes that person to conquer all throughout life. He just does not want the person walking around in pride. He wants the person to do what the definition says: *to offer* himself in a spirit of submissiveness and lowliness; not to act highminded, proud, haughty, arrogant, or assertive.

Humility is to be developed. Scripture tells us how:

"**Take my yoke upon you, and learn of me; for I am meek and lowly in heart: and ye shall find rest unto your souls**" (Mt.11:29).

Contrary to what the world thinks, humility reaps unbelievable benefits. A close study of the above verses shows this.

1.   Humility results in a person coming to Christ and learning of Him. It leads to self-evaluation, an honest and courageous evaluation. When a person looks at Jesus Christ, he sees what he should be and it motivates him to become what he should be. He sees where he needs improvement and he is driven to fill in the gaps.

2.   Humility results in conversion, assuring our entrance into the kingdom of heaven.

3.   Humility results in our being exalted by Christ in that glorious day of redemption.

4.   Humility results in healthy relationships and in community and social benefits. For example...

- It acknowledges and boosts others.
- It leads to better relationships.
- It encourages and helps others.
- It motivates others to grow and do more.

> "Be of the same mind one toward another. Mind not high things, but condescend to men of low estate. Be not wise in your own conceits" (Ro.12:16).

QUESTIONS:
1. What can you do to ward off spiritual pride and work toward a lifestyle of humility?
2. What kinds of things do you tend to take pride in? Is pride acceptable in some cases?
3. What kind of church will spiritual pride produce? Will spiritual humility produce?
4. How does a humble church leader behave?

7. THE TRAIT OF CONTROLLING SELF-INTEREST OR CONCENTRATION UPON YOURSELF (v.4).

There is the trait of controlling self-interest. Very simply, a Christian believer must forget himself. He must quit looking upon his own things, his...

- ambition
- desires
- position
- wants
- being neglected
- being overlooked
- being by-passed
- being ignored
- not being recognized
- not being honored
- not being given the position

Believers are to concentrate upon Christ and His ministry to people and reaching the world with the glorious gospel of salvation. They are not to be focused upon self. The world is too needful and too desperate for any believer to be focused upon himself. Every believer is needed to reach the lost and lonely, the shut-ins and helpless, the hungry and cold, the sinful and doomed of his community and city, country and world. Every believer does not need to be thinking on his own things, but on the things of others. He needs to be out...

- visiting
- ministering
- helping
- sharing
- feeding
- clothing
- transporting
- listening
- advising
- counseling
- planning
- teaching

> "I was a stranger, and ye took me not in: naked, and ye clothed me not: sick, and in prison, and ye visited me not" (Mt.25:43).

ILLUSTRATION:
Do you know anyone who is always focusing on himself at the expense of others? A person who is the center of his own world? Many a person has defined success as being able to climb the corporate ladder, climbing on the backs of others to get there.

To many, success is also buying a big house on the right side of town, owning new cars, and wearing the latest style of clothes that shout "Success!" But when their families fall apart or their children rebel or they fall victim to the ravages of disease, they quickly realize that material possessions matter little. The problems and tragedies of life should serve as God's wake-up call to those who focus their lives upon this world and its possessions. But will they listen? Will they lose everything that they thought was important, and lose eternity too?

PHILIPPIANS 2:1-4

What is the focus of your life? What is important to you?

> **"For what is a man profited, if he shall gain the whole world, and lose his own soul? or what shall a man give in exchange for his soul"** **(Mt.16:26).**

1. We live in a very self-centered culture. What makes a person become self-centered?
2. Are you focused upon yourself? Answer honestly. How can you focus more upon Christ and His ministry?
3. What are some things that you can do to break the mold of this culture's expectations and become Christ-centered?

SUMMARY:

Do you want to be a part of a church that learns to walk in His steps? If so, a Christian church can be a place of unity if the following traits are applied:
1. The trait of consolation
2. The trait of love
3. The trait of fellowship in the Spirit
4. The trait of compassion
5. The trait of concern for one another's joy
6. The trait of humility or lowliness of mind
7. The trait of controlling self-interest or concentration upon oneself

Let these traits become the possession of a group of Christians, and the lost will long to be with you.

PERSONAL JOURNAL NOTES:
(Reflection & Response)

1. The most important thing that I learned from this lesson was:

2. The area that I need to work on the most is:

3. I can apply this lesson to my life by:

4. Closing Statement Of Commitment:

---

[1]Gary Smalley & Dr. John Trent, *Giving The Blessing: Daily Thoughts On The Joy Of Giving.* (Nashville, TN: Thomas Nelson, 1993), March 30th entry.

	B. Humbling One's Self, 2:5-11	became obedient unto death, even the death of the cross.	to the very point of death
1. Christ is the supreme example	5 Let this mind be in you, which was also in Christ Jesus:	9 Wherefore God also hath highly exalted him, and given him a name which is above every name:	5. Christ was rewarded— highly exalted by God
2. Christ is of the very nature of God	6 Who, being in the form of God, thought it not robbery to be equal with God:	10 That at the name of Jesus every knee should bow, of things	a. Given a name above every name
3. Christ emptied Himself & became a man	7 But made himself of no reputation, and took upon him the form of a servant, and was made in the likeness of men:	in heaven, and things in earth, and things under the earth;	b. Given supreme power & authority
4. Christ humbled Himself to the point of utter humiliation—	8 And being found in fashion as a man, he humbled himself, and	11 And that every tongue should confess that Jesus Christ is Lord, to the glory of God the Father.	c. Given supreme worship as Lord

Section II
THE STEPS TO UNITY, Philippians 2:1-18

Study 2: HUMBLING ONE'S SELF

Text: Philippians 2:5-11

Aim: To learn a much needed lesson: How to let the humility of Christ flow through you.

Memory Verse:
"Let this mind be in you, which was also in Christ Jesus" (Philippians 2:5).

INTRODUCTION:
Have you ever bought something that was an imitation—it looked like the real thing but lacked the quality of the original? Chances are your imitation wore out or broke or became tarnished before too long. There is nothing like the real thing, whether it be a cherished painting, a treasured piece of jewelry, or a precious relationship. Nothing quite meets our expectations except the real thing. But there are times in life when we are supposed to try to imitate something or someone—times when we want to model ourselves after an ideal or a role model. We don't expect to be as good or perfect as the 'original,' but it is in our best interests to try. Why? Because our sinful nature is so depraved, and because we have a perfect model for all we do in Jesus Christ!

This is one of the greatest passages ever written about Jesus Christ. It paints the perfect picture of humility—the humility of Jesus Christ. No one has ever come close to humbling himself like Jesus Christ did, and no one ever will. Yet, if the problems of the church and of the world are to ever be solved, we must humble ourselves just as Christ did. The church is too often divided, too often rumbling with criticism, murmuring, differences, jealousy, envy, ambition, outside talk, negative feelings, and desires for position and recognition. The only answer is the declaration of this passage: letting the humility of Jesus Christ flow in and out of our minds. The first step to unity is letting Christ live in us. Humility is the second step to unity. The unity of a church depends upon its members walking in the humility of Jesus Christ.

PHILIPPIANS 2:5-11

OUTLINE:
1. Christ is the supreme example (v.5).
2. Christ is of the very nature of God (v.6).
3. Christ emptied Himself and became a man (v.7).
4. Christ humbled Himself to the point of utter humiliation—to the very point of death (v.8).
5. Christ was rewarded—highly exalted by God (v.9-11).

1. CHRIST IS THE SUPREME EXAMPLE (v.5).

As stated, this is one of the greatest passages ever written about Jesus Christ. Very simply, the passage says that Jesus Christ is God, yet He humbled Himself and became Man. Jesus Christ is the Person who dwelt in all the glory of perfection, but He humbled Himself and came to this corruptible world that knows little else other than selfishness, greed and death. Just imagine the enormous step down that Jesus Christ had to take to become a Man. It is utterly impossible to grasp the humility it took. Yet, this is exactly what He did and it is what we are to do. The very same *mind* that existed in Jesus Christ—that led Christ to give up everything He was and had—is to be in us. The only way the problems of the world can be solved is for every person to let the mind of Christ flood his mind. Consider the problems of…

war	selfishness	indulgence	hunger
hate	pride	extravagance	homelessness
anger	cockiness	hoarding	poverty
arguing	haughtiness	greed	disease
abuse	arrogance	stealing	jealousy
prejudice	cursing	envy	immorality

The list could go on and on. How can these problems ever be solved unless we step down from where we are to where needy people are? Unless we step down and humble ourselves—step down to where hurting people are—these problems will never be solved. Realistically, most people are not going to do this. Most people are not going to take all they are and have and get down to where the needs really are. But the Christian is to do this. This is the point of the present passage: Jesus Christ *set* and *focused His mind* upon humbling Himself. He took all He was and had and came down where we are and met our need. Now…

"Let this mind be in you, which was also in Christ Jesus" (v.5).

Take the mind of Christ and let if flow through you. Let the mind of humility and lowliness surge through your mind. Take all you are and have and get down where the needs really are. Do all you can to solve the divisiveness and cliques, grumbling and murmuring, selfish ambition and pride, desire for position and power, greed and selfishness, hurt and pain—both in the church and in the world. Humble yourself as Christ did and become part of the solution instead of the problem. Look at the mind of Christ. Lay hold of it as it is descriptively pictured in the notes that follow. *Do not miss out on the opportunity of an eternity—the glorious privilege of possessing the very mind of Christ Himself.*

ILLUSTRATION:
Every believer should cultivate the mind of Christ, that of humbling himself and going forth to meet the needs of a lost world. D.B. Rote worded it well:

"Every [believer] should cultivate a lowly spirit….No one is so much in need of a lowly spirit as servants of the Lord. It is one of the first and last qualifications for service.
"It is related of [the missionary] Francis Xavier, that as he was preaching in one of the cities of Japan, a man went up to him as if he had something to say to him privately. Xavier leaned his head near to hear what he had to say, and the scorner spit upon the face of the devoted missionary. Xavier, without a word or the least sign of annoyance, took out his pocket

handkerchief, wiped his face and went on with his important message as if nothing had happened. The scorn of the audience was turned to admiration. The most learned doctor of the city, who happened to be present, said to himself that a law which taught men such virtue, inspired them with such courage, and gave them such complete mastery over themselves, could not but be from God. Afterwards he desired baptism, and his example was followed by others....

"Learn of Me'; Jesus said, 'for I am meek and lowly in heart.'

"Though the Lord be high, yet hath He respect unto the lowly,' and 'He giveth grace unto the lowly.'

"Dear coworkers, let Christ be your Example."[1]

QUESTIONS:
1. Who is the most humble person you know? In your opinion, what qualities do they possess that make them humble? Are these qualities admirable?
2. Are there areas of your life where you need to be more humble? How can you change these areas?
3. Humility is an attitude. What kinds of things can you do to make an attitude adjustment?
4. Do you think humility comes naturally? Why or why not?

2. CHRIST IS THE VERY NATURE OF GOD (v.6).

This is critical to note, for it means...
- that Jesus Christ is not *like God*; He is God.
- that Jesus Christ did not just *achieve a high level of righteousness* when on earth, He was the very embodiment of righteousness.
- that Jesus Christ did not just *walk more perfectly* than other men walk, He was the very *picture (essence) of perfection.*
- that Jesus Christ did not become God when on earth, He has been God throughout all eternity.

Three points in this verse clearly show that Jesus Christ is God.

1. *Jesus Christ is of the "being" of God.* The word "being" means existence, what a person is within and without. This is a most glorious truth because it means that *Jesus Christ is God*; He is the very *being of God*.

> **"In the beginning was the Word, and the Word was with God, and the <u>Word was God</u>" (Jn.1:1).**

2. *Jesus Christ is in the form of God.* The word form means the permanent, constant being of a person. It is the very essence of a person, that part of him that never changes. This means a most glorious thing. Jesus is of the very essence and being and image of God. He is the divine, unchangeable God Himself. He dwells in the perfection of God and possesses the very attributes of God Himself.

> **"Who being the brightness of his glory, and the <u>express image</u> of his person, and upholding all things by the word of his power, when he had by himself purged our sins, sat down on the right hand of the Majesty on high" (Heb.1:3).**

3. *Jesus Christ is "equal with God"* (Greek). The word "equal" means to be *on an equal basis with God*; to possess all the qualities and attributes of God Himself. Note also the word "robbery" It is the picture of a thief seeking to snatch or take something that is not his. When

Jesus Christ was on earth, He was constantly claiming...
- to be God.
- to be the Son of God.
- to have the nature of God.
- to be one with God.
- to be *on an equal basis with God.*

Was He a thief? Was He robbing and snatching the title of God or was He truly God? The answer is a most glorious truth. Jesus Christ did not have to rob or snatch at equality with God. He did not have to rob and grasp after the deity of God; He was already on an equal basis with God.

"I and my Father are one" (Jn.10:30).

QUESTIONS:
1. According to Scripture, what percentage of God is Jesus Christ?
2. Why is understanding this question above important to the Christian?

3. CHRIST EMPTIED HIMSELF & BECAME A MAN (v.7).

Remember that we are dealing with the subject of humility—the fact that Jesus Christ took one great step down from heaven to earth. The step down was so great and so far that theologians do not call it *the humility of Christ, but the humiliation of Christ.* The Sovereign Lord of the universe who existed...
- in eternity and perfection
- in glory and majesty
- in dominion and power

...stepped down and became a man. But more than this: He who was the Lord and Master of the universe—who deserved all the honor and service of all living creatures—took upon Himself the form of a servant. He became the Servant of men—not only of God, but the *servant of men.* Imagine!
⇒ The Lord whom we are to serve, came and served us.
⇒ The Lord whom we are to love, came and loved us.
⇒ The Lord whom we are to adore, came and adored us.
⇒ The Lord whom we are to wait upon, came and waited upon us.
⇒ The Lord whom we are to minister to, came and ministered to us.
⇒ The Lord whom we are to seek, came and sought us.

The great distance between the majesty of Christ in heaven and the humiliation of Christ upon earth can never be measured. Our understanding of the distance would amount to no more than a small bucket of water compared to the great ocean. But we are commanded to let *the same mind of humility* flow through us; therefore, we must study the deep humility of Jesus Christ and do our best to grasp and practice it. Two statements in this verse need diligent study.
1.   Jesus Christ made Himself of no reputation; that is, He *emptied Himself.* The word "emptied" means to remove the contents of, to completely empty. It is the picture of pouring water out of a glass until it is empty or of dumping something until it is all removed.[2]. The very picture of being completely empty stirs a feeling of just how far Christ went in humbling Himself for us. What was it that was poured or emptied out of Jesus Christ when He left heaven and came to earth? (This is what theologians call the *kenosis theory.*) Note that this passage does not say. It only says that Christ *emptied Himself.* Other Scriptures, however, give some indication.
   a.   Christ did not lay aside His deity when He came to earth. He could not cease to be who He was: God. No person can ever cease to be who he is. A person may take on different traits and behave differently; a person may change his behavior and looks, but he is the same person in being, nature, and essence. Jesus Christ is God; therefore, He is always God—He always possesses the nature of God.

b. Christ laid aside some of His rights as God:

⇒ He laid aside His right *to experience only the glory* and majesty, honor and worship of heaven. In coming to earth as a man, He was to experience anything but glory and majesty, honor and worship. Men would treat Him far differently than a heavenly being.

⇒ He laid aside His right *to appear only in heaven* and to appear only as the Sovereign God of heaven. In coming to earth as a man, He was, of course, to appear as a man on earth.

As stated above, Jesus Christ emptied Himself of certain rights: the right to *appear only in heaven* and to *experience only the glory of heaven*. This is exactly what Jesus Christ Himself said when He was about to be crucified and return to heaven. He was praying to the Father when He said:

> "And now, O Father, glorify thou me with thine own self with the glory which I had with thee before the world was" (Jn.17:5).

2. Jesus Christ "**was made** in the likeness of men." The word "was made" means to become; a definite entrance into time. It is not a permanent state. Jesus became a man, but it was not to be permanent. It was only for a time, a particular period. In the fulness of time He made a definite entrance into the world as a man.

APPLICATION:

Note that Jesus Christ did not come to earth as a prince or some great leader upon earth. He did not come to receive the homage and service of men. He came as the humblest of men, as a servant to serve men. "He was brought up [humbly], probably working with his supposed father at his trade. His whole life was a life of humiliation...poverty, and disgrace; he had nowhere to lay his head, lived upon alms, was a man of sorrows and acquainted with grief, did not appear with external pomp, or any marks of distinction from other men. This was the humiliation of his life."[3]

> "But made himself of no reputation, and took upon him the form of a servant, and was made in the likeness of men" (Ph.2:7).

QUESTIONS:
1. What do you think Christ felt when He left heaven's glory for earth?
2. What did Christ empty Himself of when He was made in the likeness of men?

4. CHRIST HUMBLED HIMSELF TO THE POINT OF UTTER HUMILIATION—TO THE VERY POINT OF DEATH (v.8).

Christ humbled Himself "even [to] the death of the cross." Note two significant points.

1. Jesus Christ humbled Himself to the Father. He was obedient to God the Father. It was the Father's will for Christ to come to earth and to die for the sins of men. And Christ did it; He obeyed God the Father.

> "No man taketh it [His life] from me, but I lay it down of myself. I have power to lay it down, and I have power to take it again. This commandment have I received of my Father" (Jn.10:18).

2. Jesus Christ humbled Himself to men. He willingly allowed men to kill Him. He did not have to bear such hostile humiliation and rebellion, but He did. Just picture what is involved in the death of the cross.

⇒ Christ humbled Himself to die.

⇒ Christ humbled Himself to come out of the spiritual and eternal world (dimension) into the physical and corruptible world in order to die.

⇒ Christ humbled Himself to lay aside His eternal glory and majesty and become a man for the purpose of dying.

⇒ Christ humbled Himself to suffer rejection, denial, cursing, abuse, arrest, torture, and murder at the hands of rebellious men—whom He had originally created for the joy of eternity—rebellious men whom He had come to save.

⇒ Christ humbled Himself to take all the sins of men upon Himself and to bear the weight and suffering of them all.

⇒ Christ humbled Himself to bear the judgment and condemnation and punishment of sin for every man.

⇒ Christ humbled Himself to suffer the awful experience of having God the Father turn His back upon Him.

⇒ Christ humbled Himself to suffer the terrible justice and wrath of God against sin.

⇒ Christ humbled Himself to bear the pain of suffering for sin eternally. Christ is eternal; therefore, His death is ever before the face of God. (Just imagine! It is beyond our comprehension, but the Lord's eternal agony is fact because of the eternal nature of God.)

The discussion could go on and on, but the point is well made by Scripture. Jesus Christ not only humbled Himself to become the servant of men, He humbled Himself to suffer the ultimate degree of humiliation:

⇒ *Jesus Christ became sin for men and died as their sin before the just wrath of God.*

In a sense, hanging there upon the cross Christ was not even a man; He was the very embodiment of sin. In some way He embraced all the sin of the world and died for the sins of men.

> "For he hath made him to sin for us, who knew no sin; that we might
> be made the righteousness of God in him" (2 Cor.5:21).

APPLICATION:

Remember the point of this passage: the fact that we must let the humility of Jesus Christ flow in and through us. We are to be humble—to walk in humility before each other—to go to the extreme of humility, even if it means humiliation before each other. Why? So that the church can be unified. Unity is to prevail among us. We are to live and breathe unity. There is to be no discord in God's church:

⇒ no divisiveness   ⇒ no jealousy   ⇒ no negative truth
⇒ no grumbling   ⇒ no personal ambition   ⇒ no downing of others
⇒ no murmuring   ⇒ no self-seeking   ⇒ no air of superiority
⇒ no criticism   ⇒ no prejudice

But note: the only way we can ever know such unity is to let the mind of Christ captivate our mind. We must study, think, and learn the humility of Christ. We must let His humility flow in and through us.

> "Let nothing be done through strife or vainglory; but in lowliness of
> mind let each esteem other better than themselves. Look not every man on
> his own things, but every man also on the things of others. Let this mind
> be in you, which was also in Christ Jesus" (Ph.2:3-5).

QUESTIONS:
1. What sorts of things need to "die" in your life for you to be humbled?
2. If the above things die, what do you think will replace them?
3. Do you think that humility is related to unity? Why or why not?

5. CHRIST WAS REWARDED—HIGHLY EXALTED BY GOD (v.9-11).

Christ had humbled Himself in obedience to God the Father, and because He was faithful in being humble, God rewarded Him by exalting Him ever so highly. The point is well made: God will reward and exalt any believer who will walk as Christ walked—humbly before Him and men.

Note how highly God has rewarded and exalted Christ.

1.   God has highly honored Christ. God has given Christ a name above every name. Right now, the name of Jesus Christ is cursed all over the world. In fact, at every passing tick of the clock, the name of Jesus Christ is being cursed thousands of times by hordes of people all over the world. But note: not everyone curses His name. Some of us love His name. To us His name is the most glorious name every uttered by human voice, for His name is...

- the name that forgives our sins.

> "And that repentance and remission of sins should be preached in his name among all nations" (Lk.24:47).

- the name that gives us access into God's presence.

> "And in that day ye shall ask me nothing. Verily, verily, I say unto you, Whatsoever ye shall ask the Father in my name, he will give it you. Hitherto have ye asked nothing in my name: ask, and ye shall receive, that your joy may be full" (Jn.16:23-24).

2.   God has given Christ supreme power and authority. God has destined every knee to bow before Christ—the knees of everything in heaven and earth and under the earth. Nothing shall be exempt. The day is coming when every creature in *all the worlds and dimensions of being* shall bow their knees in subjection to the Lord Jesus Christ.

> "And hath put all things under his feet, and gave him to be the head over all things to the church" (Eph.1:22).

3.   God has given Christ supreme worship. God is going to see to it that every creature confesses that Jesus Christ is Lord to the glory of God the Father:
⇒ every nation, tongue, and language
⇒ every person, mind, and body
⇒ every race, color, and shape
⇒ every belief, creed, and religion
⇒ every man, woman, and child
⇒ every king, leader, and authority
⇒ every professional worker and laborer

Every knee shall bow and every tongue shall confess that Jesus Christ is exactly who He claimed to be: the Son of the living God. Every creature is going to worship Him as Lord, the Lord God of the universe.

> "Who shall not fear thee, O Lord, and glorify thy name? for thou only art holy: for all nations shall come and worship before thee; for thy judgments are made manifest" (Rev.15:4).

ILLUSTRATION:

No one is smart enough to fool God. Everyone will have to stand before Him one day and there will be no way to hide who we are:

> "The Queen Mary was the largest ship to cross the oceans when it was launched in 1936. Through four decades and a world war she served until she was retired, anchored as a floating hotel and museum in Long Beach, California.
> "During the conversion, her three massive smokestacks were taken off to be scraped down and repainted. But on the dock they crumbled.

PHILIPPIANS 2:5-11

"Nothing was left of the ¾-inch steel plate from which the stacks had been formed. All that remained were more than thirty coats of paint that had been applied over the years. The steel had rusted away.

"When Jesus called the Pharisees 'whitewashed tombs,' He meant they had no substance, only an exterior appearance."[A]

QUESTIONS:

1. In what ways do people "coat over" their lives in order to appear humble?
2. What has God promised to do for the person who humbles himself and seeks unity in the Church?
3. Is Jesus really Lord of your life? If you searched your heart, would there be areas where you need to be humbled, where you need to exalt Christ and not self?

A CLOSER LOOK:

Lord: means master, owner. Jesus was called *Lord* from the very first of His ministry (Mt.8:2) and He accepted the title. He even called Himself Lord (Mt.7:21). The word had been a title of respect throughout history. During the Roman empire it became the official title of Roman emperors. It was also a title given to the gods. The Hebrew title Adonai is translated Lord (Gen.15:2), so is Jehovah (Mt.1:20-22; 2:15; 3:3; 4:7, 10; 11;25; 21:9; Mk.12:29-30; Lk.1:68; 2:9). Both titles, Adonai and Jehovah, are translated Lord in Mt.22:44. Jesus Himself called God the Father, "Lord" (Mt.4:7, 10). But the title is more often given to Jesus. There is no question but that Jesus is recognized as Lord, being identical with the Old Testament Jehovah and Adonai (Mt.3:3; 12:8; 21:9; 22:43-45; Lk.1:43; Jn.14:8-10; 20:28; Acts 9:5). When Jesus is called Lord, it means that He is Master and Owner, the King of kings and Lord of lords, the only true God. He is Jehovah, Adonai, God Himself.

SUMMARY:

Christ's example of humility is a lofty one indeed. In fact, it is impossible to attain unless He fills you with His Holy Spirit every day.

A review of the lesson will remind you that:

1. Christ is the supreme example.
2. Christ is the very nature of God.
3. Christ emptied Himself & became a man.
4. Christ humbled Himself to the point of utter humiliation—to the very point of death.
5. Christ was rewarded—highly exalted by God.

PHILIPPIANS 2:5-11

PERSONAL JOURNAL NOTES:
(Reflection & Response)

1. The most important thing that I learned from this lesson was:

2. The area that I need to work on the most is:

3. This week I can apply this lesson to my life by:

4. Closing Statement of Commitment:

---

[1] D.B. Rote, Quoted in *Three Thousand Illustrations for Christian Service* by Walter B. Knight, p.366.
[2] William Barclay, *The Letters to the Philippians, Colossians, and Thessalonians* (Philadelphia, PA: Westminister Press, 1953), p.44.
[3] Matthew Henry, *Matthew Henry's Commentary*, Vol.6 (Old Tappan, NJ: Fleming H. Revell Co.), p.732f.
[4] Craig B. Larson, Editor, *Illustrations For Preaching And Teaching*, p.118.

	C. Working Out One's Own Salvation or Deliverance, 2:12-18	blameless and harmless, the sons of God, without rebuke, in the midst of a crooked and perverse nation, among whom ye shine as lights in the world;	work at being pure a. Blameless b. Harmless, sincere c. Without rebuke
1. The first work: To work out one's own salvation (deliverance) with fear & trembling	12 Wherefore, my beloved, as ye have always obeyed, not as in my presence only, but now much more in my absence, work out your own salvation with fear and trembling.	16 Holding forth the word of life; that I may rejoice in the day of Christ, that I have not run in vain, neither laboured in vain.	**5. The fifth work: To work at witnessing**
2. The second work: To work at obedience—to work out God's stirrings within the heart	13 For it is God which worketh in you both to will and to do of his good pleasure.	17 Yea, and if I be offered upon the sacrifice and service of your faith, I joy, and rejoice with you all.	**6. The sixth work: To work at following the example of sacrificial labor**
3. The third work: To work at not murmuring	14 Do all things without murmurings and disputings:	18 For the same cause also do ye joy, and rejoice with me.	
4. The fourth work: To	15 That ye may be		

Section II
THE STEPS TO UNITY, Philippians 2:1-18

Study 3:   WORKING OUT ONE'S OWN SALVATION OR DELIVERANCE

Text: Philippians 2:12-18

Aim: To learn the practical duties of the Christian life: What you need to do *after* you have been saved.

Memory Verse:
    "For it is God which worketh in you both to will and to do of His good pleasure" (Philippians 2:13).

INTRODUCTION:
    There are some Christians whose lives are like a "parked car"—if God wants them to move down the road of life He will have to push them Himself.
    Others live the Christian life by keeping a car washed and polished—however they fail to give proper attention to the engine that supplies the power.
    And still, there are others who live the Christian life by holding the steering wheel and patiently waiting for instructions on where and when to go. Their car has been gassed up by the presence of the Holy Spirit who freely gives His power and counsel for the journey ahead: A lifetime of adventure in the Spirit!
    Are you like that parked car? Waiting for a push?
    Or can your life be described as one that looks good on the outside but lacks power on the inside?
    The goal of this lesson is to learn how to sit in God's presence and use His power and counsel in order to work out our salvation. The only thing that the Lord will not provide is a decision to sit behind the wheel and drive the car. This is a choice of the will that each one of us must make.
    This passage is still dealing with unity—unity in the church and unity among believers. But the passage is unique because it brings up the great subject of salvation. Keep in mind that sal-

vation means deliverance and that salvation is of God. It is God who has saved and delivered you: "For by grace are ye saved" (Eph.2:8-9). But once you are saved, go to work—work out your own salvation and deliverance. Salvation is not stagnant and complacent. A saved person is not to be sitting around doing nothing and letting the chips fall where they may. A saved person is to get up and go to work. He is to do all he can to work out his own deliverance. This is the subject of the present passage. If the church is to be unified—if believers are to walk in a spirit of unity, then they must look at their salvation—at the whole scope of their lives and the glorious salvation God has given them—and they must do all they can to work out their own deliverance.

OUTLINE:
1. The first work: to work out one's own salvation (deliverance) with fear and trembling (v.12).
2. The second work: to work at obedience—to work out the stirrings of God within the heart (v.13).
3. The third work: to work at not murmuring (v.14).
4. The fourth work: to work at being pure (v.15).
5. The fifth work: to work at witnessing (v.16).
6. The sixth work: to work at following the example of sacrificial labor (v.17-18).

1. THE FIRST WORK: TO WORK OUT ONE'S SALVATION (DELIVERANCE) WITH FEAR AND TREMBLING (VS 12).

Remember Paul is in prison being held on false charges. There is a good chance he will be executed. He is not sure he will ever see and share with the Philippians again. Therefore, what he is now writing is carefully chosen. So far as he knows, these words could be his last words to the Philippian church. This is the reason we need to pay close attention to the instructions.

What does it mean to work out your own salvation? The word "work out" means to complete the effort and the work begun; to accomplish it perfectly; to bring it to completion. The point is: do not go half-way in salvation. Do not take bits and pieces when there is a whole parcel. Do not be satisfied with a little when you can have much. Grow until salvation is completed in you. It is *your own* salvation. No friend, no pastor can work it out for you. You alone must do it.

The point is clearly stated: once God has saved a person, that person is to get busy obeying God. He is to take hold of the new life and salvation God has given him, and he is to work on it until it is completed and finished, that is, until God takes him home and perfects it.

Note that the Philippians are an excellent example. Paul says that they had always obeyed God, not only when he was with them but also when he was away. Now, as he was facing death, he wanted them more than ever to work out their salvation—to continue obeying God until their salvation was completed and perfected.

Note also the words "fear and trembling." Life is not a bed of roses. It is full of trial, pain, hurt, tragedy, disease, accident, loss, temptation, sin, evil, corruption, and death. Every human being experiences such things until he comes face to face with death. Life is sometimes beautiful and wonderful, but reality is what has just been listed: life is a journey of trials until the point of death. No amount of denial or camouflage can hide or escape the fact. The only thing that can bring abundance of life is the *absolute confidence* that we shall live eternally in a perfect world. What is the point of mentioning all this? The point is forceful: we are expected to work out our own salvation and to do it with fear and trembling.

⇒ We are to fear and tremble because of the trials and temptations of life. Anyone of them can throw us or cause us to buckle under. The world and its temptations and trials are strong, and the flesh is weak. We can slip into sin and failure before we know it unless we are constantly working out our deliverance—fearing and trembling lest we fail.

⇒ We are to fear and tremble lest we disappoint the Lord. He has saved us, and He has gone to the ultimate limit in order to do it. He has demonstrated a perfect love for us by taking all our sins upon Himself and bearing our punishment for us. Therefore, when we sin and fail, it cuts His heart to no end. For His sake—to keep from hurting Him—we must work out our salvation, fearing and trembling lest we cut His heart again.

⇒ We are to fear and tremble because we are to face the judgment seat of Christ. If we sin, we shall be judged and judged severely. Though we may try to reason away the fact, our thoughts about the judgment of God do not affect God's judgment one iota. Every one of us who sins and fails to work out his own salvation shall be judged and suffer loss—great loss. Scripture teaches nothing else. For this reason, the reason of judgment, we must work out our salvation—work it out with fear and trembling.

> **"And fear not them which kill the body, but are not able to kill the soul: but rather fear him which is able to destroy both soul and body in hell" (Mt.10:28).**

ILLUSTRATION:
Have you ever felt weary and worn, as though you were being stretched and pulled in every direction at once, like you were going to snap? Listen to this man's story...

Jimmy was ready for the race of his life. His day had finally arrived. He was ready to compete at the peak of his ability and performance. As with any qualified athlete, his training had not begun on race day. It had started years ago when he had committed his body to undergo a strenuous training program. Daily, he had stretched and lifted weights. He had spent hours running and running. He had disciplined his mind to eat only the right food. Many times during the process, he had wished for an easier, less painful training session and program.

Had he wanted to quit? Almost always. Was it easy? Never. Then why did he do it? As Sherlock Holmes would say: *"Elementary Watson. He did it because he wanted to win the race!"*

Are you properly preparing for the race of your life? Are you training and working out your salvation day by day with fear and trembling? Are you even in the race? God wants you to be in His training program. It worked for Paul—and it will work for you.

> **"I have fought a good fight, I have finished my course, I have kept the faith" (2 Tim.4:7).**

Christian believer, this is a race that you have to win!

QUESTIONS:
1. In what area(s) are you being stretched by God at the present time?
2. Every Christian believer should set reasonable goals for working out his own salvation, for growing in Christ. What goals do you have this year for the following:
   a. A daily time of worship, of Bible study and prayer
   b. Bible memorization of key verses
   c. Sharing the gospel with an unbeliever
   d. A ministry of encouragement
   e. Discipling a young believer
   f. An accountable relationship with God and others Christians

2. THE SECOND WORK: TO WORK AT OBEDIENCE—TO WORK OUT GOD'S STIRRINGS WITHIN THE HEART (v.13).

The second work of salvation is to obey.

> **"It is God which worketh in you both to will and to do of his good pleasure" (v.13).**

The word "worketh" means to energize. God arouses, stirs, and energizes the heart of the believer to do His will. This is a wonderful truth. Just think about it: we all experience movements and stirrings within our heart toward God. God is working within us—energizing us—giving us both *the will and power* to do what pleases Him. Our duty is to grab hold of the stirrings—not to let them pass.

APPLICATION:
God does not leave us alone to work out our salvation and deliverance. God uses the energy and stirring to direct and guide us. The point to see is that God is forever working within us— never leaving us alone—working and moving us to complete our salvation.

The tragedy is this: we sometimes ignore, neglect, and refuse to respond to the movement of God. When we feel the stirrings, we desperately need to respond and do whatever God is arousing us to do. How often do we continue to sit or go about our own affairs instead of heeding the working and stirrings of God? How complacent and lethargic we are? Just think how much growth we lose and how often we must cut the heart of God to the core—all because we choose the things, possessions, and activities of this world instead of responding to the stirrings and direction of God.

> "It is the spirit that quickeneth; the flesh profiteth nothing: the words that I speak unto you, they are spirit, and they are life" (Jn.6:63).

God will always meet us right where we are. He has never called any of us to be "super saints." He knows that we have feet of clay and that because of sin we are programed for failure. But take heart! He has promised His help as we work out our salvation.

QUESTIONS:
1. What kind of work do you need Him to do for you right now?
2. According to Scripture, how does God help His children obey Him?
3. Finish this statement: It is hard for me to obey God when ...

3. THE THIRD WORK: TO WORK AT NOT MURMURING (v.14).

The word "murmuring" means to mutter, grumble, and complain. Note: it means the quiet, soft, behind-the-back, undertone of murmuring and grumbling. It is the kind of criticism, dissatisfaction, fault-finding and gossip that goes on within small groups or cliques.

The word "disputings" means arguments, outward and vocal questionings, and expressions of doubt.

Note several significant facts.

1. Murmurings and disputes are not to be allowed in the church. As the verse says: *all things* are to be done without murmurings and disputings. If murmuring begins among a clique or even between two people, the spiritual leaders of the church are to deal with it just as Christ laid out. It is not to be allowed to fester. Murmurings, unless they are stopped, will lead to disputes, turmoil, and divisiveness.

2. Murmuring and disputes are *never of God—never*! This is the very point of this charge. *All things*—nothing is left out—are to be done without murmuring and disputes.

3. Murmuring and disputes were the very sins that brought judgment upon so many Jews in the wilderness wanderings of Israel.

> "Neither murmur ye, as some of them also murmured, and were destroyed of the destroyer" (1 Cor.10:10; cp. Num.20:2f; 21:4).

4. The person who murmurs and disputes is not working at his salvation or deliverance. He is doing the very opposite: working to bring judgment upon himself.

ILLUSTRATION:

Have you ever been a victim of murmuring? Do you remember what it felt like? You probably had feelings of hurt and anger and a determination to protect yourself—like in this example:

"Betrayed!" The once transparent member of the neighborhood church was crushed. Sue had been so open to trust other Christians with her personal struggles. She had always been taught to share her burdens, but how could anyone take her personal pain and make it the talk of the church grape-vine? "Never again will I trust my heart with another person," she vowed. And at that very moment, another member of the body of Christ withdrew into a hard shell of isolation: another victim of murmuring and gossip.

APPLICATION:

The results of murmuring are far worse than people ever think. This is the primary reason God forbids murmuring and disputes in no uncertain terms. Murmuring...

- hurts
- damages
- divides
- tears down
- misleads people

- opposes God's will
- hinders progress
- stymies growth
- elevates selfish opinion

- is self-centered
- says "look at me"
- pushes people away from Christ & the church

> "For I fear, lest, when I come, I shall not find you such as I would, and that I shall be found unto you such as ye would not: lest there be debates, envyings, wraths, strifes, backbitings, whisperings, swellings, tumults" (2 Cor.12:20).

QUESTIONS:
1. What practical things can you do to stop murmuring when you hear it happening?
2. What is it about murmuring that makes it one of the devil's favorite tools to use on a Christian?

4. THE FOURTH WORK: TO WORK AT BEING PURE (V.15).

Believers are to work out their salvation by working at being pure.

1. Believers are to work at being "blameless": free from fault and censure, above reproach and rebuke. The believer is to live a blameless and pure life, both in the church and in the world. No one is to be able to point to the Christian and accuse or blame him for anything. The Christian is to be clean, unpolluted, spotless, holy, righteous, and pure before man and God.

2. Believers are to work at being harmless: unmixed and unadulterated. It is the idea of flour or grain passing through a sieve to separate the pure from the impure. It means that our thoughts and lives...

- are not to be polluted by watching, reading, and listening to worldly and sexual attractions.
- are not to be given over to worldly and sexual attractions.

Our thoughts and lives are to be pure, clean, uncontaminated, and unpolluted.

> "I would have you wise unto that which is good, and simple [harmless] concerning evil" (Ro.16:19).

3. Believers are to work at being "without rebuke": without blemish, spot, or defect. This is a word that is taken from the Old Testament sacrifices made to God. The idea is that the believer is to live and walk upon earth under the eyes and scrutiny of God. He is to walk without any blemish, spot, or defect.

However, note a fact: the believer lives in a crooked and perverse generation. The world is wicked and evil, twisted and perverted; therefore, the believer has a difficult path to walk. But he is to be the light of the world. He is to reflect the purity and holiness of God Himself.

> **"Ye are the light of the world. A city that is set on an hill cannot be hid" (Mt.5:14).**

ILLUSTRATION:
The theory that is used for mixing paint at a hardware store is really quite simple: the more colored tint that you add to the can of white paint, the darker the paint will become.

It only takes a drop of black tint to change the color of pure white to off-white. Once that first drop of tint goes into the can of white paint, it can never be taken out. That can of paint will never be pure white again; it can only get darker.

A Christian can work at being pure. True, sin is sin and that cannot be denied. But unlike the tainted can of white paint, the Christian has hope in this great truth: *"Create in me a clean heart and renew a right spirit within me"* (Ps.51:10).

Literally, God makes something out of nothing and gives to people who are truly repentant of their sins a brand new start. In other words, He forgets about the impure can of paint and gives us a brand new can of white paint. *"Though our sins be as scarlet, He makes us as white as snow"* (Is.1:18).

QUESTIONS:
1. What sorts of things can cause a blemish or spot on your pure life?
2. Can you remember a time when God gave you a brand new start?
3. How can we realistically be *in* the world but not *of* the world?

5. THE FIFTH WORK: TO WORK AT WITNESSING (v.16).

The wording of this verse is descriptive: "Holding forth the word of life." It means to offer the gospel to all that will listen. Imagine! There is a *Word of life* that allows men to live forever. Men never have to die.

⇒ It is like saying the fountain of youth has been discovered with one difference: the Word of life not only brings eternal youth, it brings perfection—a perfect world and a perfect life.
⇒ It is like saying the cure for cancer has been discovered with one difference: the Word of life not only cures the cancer, it injects the energy of everlasting life into the other cells of the body.

But note the terrible tragedy! So many of us do not hold forth the Word of life. We hold back. We do not share the message of the glorious gospel of life. The Word of life is just what it says: it is the message of life that is in Christ Jesus our Lord.

> **"I am come that they might have life, and that they might have it more abundantly" (Jn.10:10).**

ILLUSTRATION:
It was during a recent short-term missions trip that the power of the gospel was seen in a fresh light. The businessman was seen walking into a park where he stationed himself and began to tell the story of Jesus Christ to a small group of people. The businessman was not a professional preacher by any means, but he made himself available for the Lord's work. He simply had a firm grasp on this truth: *"God does not call the qualified. He qualifies the called."*

"The people in the park just kept gathering around me as I was sharing the gospel of Jesus Christ." *"Do you want me to explain the gospel to you also?"* he would ask the newest members of the group as they would walk in closer. On that particular day, numbers of young people gave their hearts to Jesus; just because one unqualified man accepted the call from the God who qualifies the called.

APPLICATION:
The one thing we must work at is holding forth the Word of life, the gospel of salvation. The Word of life is the only hope for a world that reels under the weight of so many desperate needs, especially the desperate need to handle sin and evil and the terrible destiny of death.

> "But sanctify the Lord God in your hearts: and be ready always to give an answer to every man that asketh you a reason of the hope that is in you with meekness and fear" (1 Pt.3:15).

QUESTIONS:
1. When was the last time you shared the gospel, the Word of life, with someone?
2. Why do so many believers fail to witness, fail to share the gospel?
3. Who will you see this week who needs to hear the gospel?

6. THE SIXTH WORK: TO WORK AT FOLLOWING THE EXAMPLE OF SACRIFICIAL LABOR (v.17-18).

Very simply stated, Paul had offered himself as a sacrifice to serve men. The picture is that of the sacrifice and offerings made by people to the heathen gods. Paul had taken his body and offered it as a sacrifice and service for people. He lived for nothing else except to hold forth the Word of life to people. His body was totally sacrificed for that purpose and that purpose alone.

> "And he said to them all, If any man will come after me, let him deny himself, and take up his cross daily, and follow me" (Lk.9:23).

APPLICATION:
Today's culture has little comprehension of Biblical sacrifice. The conventional wisdom of the day gives everyone the go-ahead to be happy, no matter what it costs. We often fail to thank God for the blessings He gives us; but more importantly, we fail to remember the price that was paid to bring us the glorious message of salvation, the sacrifice paid by both Christ and our forefathers.

QUESTIONS:
1. Biblical sacrifice is a reality in the life of the committed Christian. What kinds of sacrifices can you make for the sake of the church and the people of the earth?
2. Is your lifestyle of service and labor an encouragement or a stumblingblock to others? Explain your answer.

SUMMARY:

As you work out your salvation, remember that the Christian has six items of work to do in working out his own salvation or deliverance:
1. To work out his own salvation with fear and trembling
2. To work at obedience
3. To work at not murmuring
4. To work at being pure
5. To work at witnessing
6. To work at following the example of sacrificial labor

PHILIPPIANS 2:12-18

PERSONAL JOURNAL NOTES:
(Reflection & Response)

1. The most important thing that I learned from this lesson was:

2. The area that I need to work on the most is:

3. I can apply this lesson to my life by:

4. Closing Statement Of Commitment:

	III. THE EXAMPLES OF SOME CHRISTIAN BELIEVERS, 2:19-30	likeminded, who will naturally care for your state.	brotherly spirit in caring for others
		20 For all seek their own, not the things which are Jesus Christ's.	3. He was willing to deny himself--to be obsessed with the things of Christ
	A. The Example of Timothy--a Young Man Who Willingly Served In Second Place, 2:19-24	21 But ye know the proof of him, that, as a son with the father, he hath served with me in the gospel.	4. He was willing to be a son, a disciple
a. Willing to be tried & proven
		22 Him therefore I hope to send present-	b. Willing to go as sent
1. Timothy--a young man who willingly served in second place	19 But I trust in the Lord Jesus to send Timotheus shortly unto you, that I also may be of good comfort, when I know your state.	ly, so soon as I shall see how it will go with me.
23 But I trust in the	
2. He had a kindred,	20 For I have no man	Lord that I also myself shall come shortly.	

Section III
THE EXAMPLES OF SOME CHRISTIAN BELIEVERS, Philippians 2:19-30

Study 1: **THE EXAMPLE OF TIMOTHY—A YOUNG MAN WHO WILLINGLY SERVED IN SECOND PLACE**

Text: **Philippians 2:19-24**

Aim: To make a permanent decision to serve wherever God calls you.

Memory Verse:
> "Not that I speak in respect of want: for I have learned, in whatsoever state I am, therewith to be content" (Philippians 4:11).

INTRODUCTION:

The competitive culture in which we live scorns being "number two." It is seen as a failure to measure up to acceptable standards of excellence.

A national car rental firm has attempted to place a postive spin on being number two. For in their eyes, "number two tries harder." In other words, number two will always be seeking to excel. They will stay responsive to the customers. They will not get lazy. You can count on number two to get the job done for you.

In the same sense, when God calls a 'Timothy' to serve as *number two*, He expects him to serve willingly. It takes a special person to serve in a support capacity. None of us can do it until God calls us and equips us to serve.

Nothing challenges the human heart any more than the faithful example of others. This passage gives us the dynamic example of a man who was totally committed to Jesus Christ: Timothy. Timothy was a young man who willingly served in second place.

OUTLINE:
1. Timothy—a young man who willingly served in second place (v.19).
2. He had a kindred, brotherly spirit in caring for others (v.20).
3. He was willing to deny himself—to be obsessed with the things of Christ (v.21).
4. He was willing to be a son, a disciple (v.22-24).

1. TIMOTHY, A YOUNG MAN WHO WILLINGLY SERVED IN SECOND PLACE (v.19).

The scene is this. Paul is deeply concerned about the Philippian church and its believers. He loves them deeply and he longs to minister among them. Note that his pastoral heart reaches out to them: he mentions their welfare twice:
⇒ He wants to know their state or condition (v.19).
⇒ He wants to care for them (v.20).
But he is in prison; he cannot personally visit the church. What can he do? He does the next best thing. He plans to send his faithful companion and co-worker, Timothy, just as soon as he can.

The point to note is the pastoral heart of both Paul and Timothy, especially Timothy, for he is the subject of these verses. Timothy was a man who was called to serve in second place. However, of all the persons covered in Scripture, Timothy was as faithful to the Lord as any. He willingly and sacrificially served in second place.

APPLICATION:
Serving in second place is a privilege. The second man not only leads those under his responsibility, but he also contributes to the life and ministry of the first man.

QUESTIONS:
1. The ability to be content is one of life's keys for the Christian. Whether number one or number two, what makes a Christian content in his or her job?
2. What kinds of sacrifices does a "number two" person make?
3. Have you ever been a "number two" person? What inward struggles does a "number two" person have to resolve?

2. HE HAD A KINDRED, BROTHERLY SPIRIT IN CARING FOR OTHERS (v.20).

There were many excellent ministers of the gospel, but Timothy's spirit came closest to Paul's than all the others. Timothy cared for the churches and their believers just as Paul cared. His care arose from deep within: it was genuine and sincere—the same kind of care that a genuine brother would have.

> "And I will give you pastors according to mine heart, which shall feed you with knowledge and understanding" (Jer.3:15).

ILLUSTRATION:
Timothy's position with Paul was more than a job: it was his life. He had a genuine concern for people. Listen to this conversation between two lay teachers, one of whom had grown weary of teaching:
"Well, how is it going for you in your Bible class?"
"Going well, thank you. And how are things in your Bible class?"
"Well, I love teaching and studying. I love the class socials and fellowship meetings we have. And I love the teaching conferences our church sends us to every year. I love it all except one thing."
"Which is?"

"The visiting. The church wants me to visit every class member, and I just do not have the time to become involved in their lives and problems. Some of them have already called me to share their problems and illnesses at all hours of the day and evening. And, frankly, I just do not have the time to visit and give them the attention needed."

"I know where you are coming from. But I need to remind you of one important detail: Without the people, there would be no Bible class and no church and no witness for Christ upon the earth. Can you imagine what the earth would be like without the witness of Christ? Your witness and gift of teaching is needed. I hope you will continue and somehow make time to visit and care for your class."

QUESTIONS:
1. Timothy had a real concern for people. But people who serve in the church serve for a lot of reasons. What are some things that motivate you to serve?
2. Who do you know that needs your help or service?
3. Does God expect us all to serve, or just the church staff?
4. What would happen if everyone in your church got involved in outreach and ministry?

3. HE WAS WILLING TO DENY HIMSELF—TO BE OBSESSED WITH THE THINGS OF CHRIST (v.21).

In no uncertain terms, Paul says:

> "**All** seek their own, not the things which are Jesus Christ's" (v.21).

Paul was referring to the ministers of that day, but it is a sweeping indictment of believers in all generations!

Lehman Strauss states:
> *"There are so few who devote their lives in selfless service. We are more concerned with our interests, our goods, our getting ahead, than we are with the needs of others....Few are seeking to follow closely in the steps of Christ and of Christlike men such as Paul. Most of us seek our own interests while we profess Christ's Name."*[1]

The point is well made: Timothy did not seek his own things. He denied himself. He had not fallen into the trap of so many. His primary concern was for the mission and truth of Christ and the welfare of the church. But this was not true with most of the believers and ministers in Rome, and tragically, it has not been true with many believers and ministers down through the centuries. Many have sought their own things first; many have made the things of Christ second in order to protect their...

- livelihood
- comfort
- acceptance
- security
- recognition
- position
- authority
- friendships
- following
- support
- possessions

> "**Jesus said unto him, If thou wilt be perfect, go and sell that thou hast, and give to the poor, and thou shalt have treasure in heaven: and come and follow me**" (Mt.19:21).

APPLICATION:
Selfishness and greed are seen early in our lives. As little babies, we want the toy another baby is holding. Growing older only has refined our obsession with material things.

QUESTIONS:
1. Everyone who is a Christian believer should have Timothy's willingness to deny himself and serve others. In practical terms, how can you learn to serve others?

2. Do you think God understands when some believers say they are just too busy to serve? Why or why not?
3. What are the reasons you serve? Do you sometimes find yourself making excuses instead of of making commitments?

4. HE WAS WILLING TO BE A SON, A DISCIPLE (v.22-24).

There was a close bond between Paul and Timothy. Timothy was as a son to Paul, and note: Timothy looked upon Paul as a father. Paul could never have said this if Timothy thought and acted otherwise.

Paul enlisted Timothy as one of his disciples and missionary partners on his second missionary journey. From that time forth, Timothy became a dynamic minister of the Lord—a minister who was called to serve in second place.

1.   Timothy was a close companion of Paul.
      a.   Paul called Timothy his son in the faith (1 Cor.4:17).
      b.   Timothy was with Paul...
            • in Philippi (Acts 16:1f).
            • in Thessalonica and Berea (Acts 17:1-14).
            • in Corinth (Acts 18:1-5).
            • in Ephesus (Acts 19:21-22).
            • in prison in Rome (Col.1:1; Ph.1:1).
2.   Timothy was involved in one way or another with seven of the writings of Paul.
      ⇒ Corinthians   ⇒ Colossians and Philippians
      ⇒ Romans (he sends greetings to   ⇒ 1 and 2 Thessalonians
         the church)   ⇒ 1 and 2 Timothy

3.   Timothy was closely connected to Paul in ministering to the churches. Timothy was sent by Paul to minister...
      • in Thessalonica (1 Th.3:6).
      • in Corinth (1 Cor.4:17; 16:10-11).
      • in Philippi (Ph.2:19).

APPLICATION:
The point to see is how closely bound together Paul and Timothy were and how faithful Timothy was. He was a tried and proven minister, a minister willing to serve in the place the Lord had put him—the position of serving in second place.
      ⇒ Not every one can serve in first place; there aren't enough positions!
      ⇒ Not every one is gifted to serve in first place.
      ⇒ Not every one is called to serve in first place.
      ⇒ Not every one is willing to serve in first place.

ILLUSTRATION:
The reason that Paul and Timothy were able to work so well together was because of their friendship. This story from the classroom illustrates the importance of Christian friendships.

> "'Is it true,' asked a student, 'that all the people in the world could live in Texas?' 'Yes,' replied the professor, 'if they were friends.' And if they were not friends even the world itself is too small."

Paul and Timothy's commitment of friendship advanced the cause of Christ not only to Texas, but to the entire world.

What *is important* is this:
1. Where can you serve?
2. What are you gifted to do?
3. Where has God called you to serve?
4. Are you willing to serve?

> "Let a man so account of us, as of the ministers of Christ, and stewards of the mysteries of God" (1 Cor.4:1).

SUMMARY:

You have learned to observe the qualities that Timothy had in order to serve as "number two." In review, they are:
1. Timothy was a young man who willingly served in second place.
2. He had a kindred, brotherly spirit in caring for others.
3. He was willing to deny himself—to be obsessed with the things of Christ.
4. He was willing to be a son, a disciple.

Timothy was *willing*...are you?

PERSONAL JOURNAL NOTES:
(Reflection & Response)

1. The most important thing that I learned from this lesson was:

2. The area that I need to work on the most is:

3. I can apply this lesson to my life by:

4. Closing Statement Of Commitment:

---

[1]Lehman Strauss, *Devotional Studies in Philippians* (Neptune, NJ: Loizeaux Brothers, 1959), p.133.
[2]*The Homilope* [church envelope], Quoted in *Three Thousand Illustrations for Christian Service* by Walter B. Knight, p.300.

	B. The Example of Epaphroditus--a Man Who Was Not a Quitter Nor a Coward, 2:25-30	but God had mercy on him; and not on him only, but on me also, lest I should have sorrow upon sorrow.	
1. He did not quit nor forsake his brother	25 Yet I supposed it necessary to send to you Epaphroditus, my brother, and companion in labour, and fellowsoldier, but your messenger, and he that ministered to my wants.	28 I sent him therefore the more carefully, that, when ye see him again, ye may rejoice, and that I may be the less sorrowful.	4. Conclusion: The appeal
2. He did not quit nor forsake the church	26 For he longed after you all, and was full of heaviness, because that ye had heard that he had been sick.	29 Receive him therefore in the Lord with all gladness; and hold such in reputation:	a. Paul is sending him back to the church so the church can rejoice in him
3. He did not quit nor forsake God	27 For indeed he was sick nigh unto death:	30 Because for the work of Christ he was nigh unto death, not regarding his life, to supply your lack of service toward me.	b. Receive him: He builds his reputation; he gambles & risks his life for Christ

Section III
THE EXAMPLES OF SOME CHRISTIAN BELIEVERS,
Philippians 2:19-30

Study 2:   THE EXAMPLE OF EPAPHRODITUS—A MAN WHO WAS NOT A QUITTER NOR A COWARD

Text: Philippians 2:25-30

Aim: To make one great promise to Christ: To never quit.

Memory Verse:
> "Therefore, my beloved brethren, be ye stedfast, unmoveable, always abounding in the work of the Lord, forasmuch as ye know that your labour is not in vain in the Lord (1 Cor.15:58).

INTRODUCTION:
Have things ever gotten so bad that you just wanted to quit? If we are truthful, all of us would admit to having these kind of thoughts at some point in our lives. Listen to this lesson from history:

"Never, never, never give up," Winston Churchill shouted before the parliament of England. After repeating these passionate words to a post-World War II college graduating class, Churchill, the great British leader, returned to his seat and sat down.

Churchill could speak from personal experience, for he was the great prime minister of England when England was at the mercy of Hitler's German war machine. Facing seemingly insurmountable odds, he rallied his fellow countrymen to be courageous and fight for the cause of freedom.

Under Churchill's leadership, the flow of history was changed. England, with her allies, was able to overcome and defeat the Axis powers. Many historians credit Churchill's leader ship as a key to victory. He refused to lose. He refused to quit. And his courage was contagious.

If you are on the edge of despair and ready to quit, remember: never, never, never give up!

William Barclay points to a dramatic story behind Epaphroditus. The Philippian church had heard that Paul was in prison and that he was having an extremely difficult time. Their hearts went out to him, so they decided to do two things: to take up an offering to meet Paul's material needs and to send a dedicated layman who could remain with him to help him. Such a man would have to be savagely brave, for by attaching himself to a man facing a capital crime, he would be leaving himself open to the charge of being an accomplice. By helping Paul, the man would be risking his own life. The man chosen was Epaphroditus.

While in Rome, Epaphroditus fell seriously ill and came close to death. News of his illness reached Philippi. And in turn, news returned to Epaphroditus that his home church was worried over his welfare. He in turn began to worry over them. But God spared him; and after gaining his strength, Paul felt for some reason (perhaps to keep this illness from recurring or to eliminate the possibility of his being arrested) that Epaphroditus should return to Philippi.

But the possibility of a problem existed. If he returned before Paul's fate was known, some would call him a quitter, a coward, a failure. The answer to this criticism is the very reason for this passage. Paul gives a glowing appraisal of their messenger.

OUTLINE:
1. He did not quit nor forsake his brother (v.25).
2. He did not quit nor forsake the church (v.26).
3. He did not quit nor forsake God (v.27).
4. Conclusion: the appeal to joy and to receive the person who is not a quitter (v.28-30).

1. HE DID NOT QUIT NOR FORSAKE HIS BROTHER (v.25).

Epaphroditus had been sent to Rome to minister to Paul who was in prison. Epaphroditus became critically ill, almost dying. He could have easily returned to Philippi after he recovered, but he did not. He stuck to his call and mission, and he completed it. Epaphroditus was so staunch a believer that Paul gave him five titles.

1. He was a *Christian brother*. Note the tenderness: Paul called him "my brother." A brother is a person who has the same parent. Epaphroditus was born of God. He had placed his faith and trust in the Lord Jesus Christ, and God had honored his faith by giving him a new birth—a spiritual birth. God had made a *new creature* or *new man* out of him (2 Cor.5:17; Eph.4:24; Col.3:10). Therefore, he was a brother to Paul and a member of God's family.

> **"But as many as received him, to them gave he power to become the sons of God, even to them that believe on his name" (Jn.1:12).**

2. He was a *companion in the work of the Lord*. Many persons serve in the work of the Lord, but not everyone is a true companion in labor. A true companion is *by the side* of his friend; he is there with him: understanding, feeling, supporting, consoling, comforting, encouraging, and helping whenever needed. There is nothing between true companions...

- no distance
- no envy
- no withdrawal
- no competition
- no neglect
- no forsaking

Paul was a prisoner about to stand trial for his life, and he had been forsaken by most believers (2 Tim.4:16). But note Epaphroditus: he stood by Paul despite the severe circumstances. And remember: he had become deathly ill; but even then, when he had every reason to return home for recuperation, he stayed in Rome by Paul's side.

"Greater love hath no man than this, that a man lay down his life for his friends. Ye are my friends, if ye do whatsoever I command you" (Jn.15:13-14).

3. He was a *fellowsoldier*. No doubt this refers to the hardiness and stedfastness of Epaphroditus. By sticking so closely to Paul, he ran the risk of being identified as a follower of Paul who was being falsely tried as an insurrectionist against the state. This danger was probably the reason so many believers forsook Paul (2 Tim.4:16). But not Epaphroditus; he stood fast—he stood as a fellowsoldier with Paul...
- despite the danger.
- despite his own ill health.

Epaphroditus was set on completing his ministry and on helping Paul in his ministry as much as possible—despite the terrible circumstances of imprisonment and illness that drug him to the brink of death. Epaphroditus was a true soldier—willing to risk his life for the sake of the gospel of God's people.

"Thou therefore endure hardness, as a good soldier of Jesus Christ. No man that warreth entangleth himself with the affairs of this life; that he may please him who hath chosen him to be a soldier" (2 Tim.2:3-4).

4. He was *a messenger of the church*. The word "messenger" is the very word for apostle. The word means an ambassador sent on a very special mission. Paul is saying that this dear saint of God had been called as a very special messenger and ambassador for God. He was far from being a quitter! Far from being a coward!

5. He was *a very special minister*. William Barclay points out that this word would have great meaning to the Greek minds of the Philippian church. The word was used only of great men. The title was bestowed only upon great benefactors, men who loved their city, culture, arts, or sports so much that they gave huge sums of money to support these functions. The person was looked upon as a great servant or minister given over to his cause. Paul is here bestowing the great title of *minister* upon Epaphroditus. Epaphroditus was an extraordinary minister of God who ministered to Paul's needs.

"Even as the Son of man came not to be ministered unto, but to minister, and to give his life a ransom for many" (Mt.20:28).

QUESTIONS:
1. The bond we have with Christian brothers and sisters should be stronger than what we have with our own blood brothers and sisters. This includes our level of commitment to them. Why?
2. Who are your most trusted friends?
3. What qualities do they have that allows you to trust them?
4. How can we develop the kind of bond and commitment that we would have with our Christian brothers and sisters?

2. HE DID NOT QUIT NOR FORSAKE THE CHURCH (v.26).

The Philippian church had sent Epaphroditus to help and minister to Paul. While there in Rome he had become deathly sick. At that point, Epaphroditus could have forsaken the mission of the church. He could have concluded that the mission was not worth losing his life over and returned home. The threat of being identified as a cohort of Paul would have been understood and accepted by many if not all, and his illness and the need to recuperate from a deathly illness would have definitely been understood by all. Epaphroditus had every human reason to return home, letting someone else take up the gauntlet and resume the task.

But as a true soldier of Jesus Christ, he would not, and he did not. In fact, note the glorious testimony of this verse. Epaphroditus was not concerned over his welfare but over the church's welfare. News of his illness had reached the church back home, and Epaphroditus was concerned about his family, friends, and the church's worrying over him. What a heart of tenderness, warmth, softness, and ministry! Just the kind of heart we all need.

The point to note is this: Epaphroditus was faithful to his call and to his church. He did not quit nor forsake the church. He had every reason to do so, but he did not. He stood fast despite the worst kind of circumstances and the threat to his own life.

ILLUSTRATION:

Today, we are living in a culture that shrinks back from commitments. Most people (by far most) are non-commital. George Barna points this out in eight striking facts. These are...

*** Signs of Reduced Commitments In Life ***
(America, 1990)

1. The divorce rate is climbing: half of all new marriages will end in divorce.
2. Adults feel they have fewer close friends than did adults in past decades.
3. Brand loyalty in consumer purchasing studies has dropped in most product categories, and by as much as 60% in some categories.
4. The proportion of people willing to join an organization is declining in relation to churches, labor unions, political parties, clubs, and community associations.
5. Book clubs and record clubs are less likely to attract new members when multiple-year or multi-product commitments were required.
6. The percentage of adults who sense a duty to fight for their country, regardless of the cause, has dropped.
7. The percentage of people who commit to attend events but fail to show is on the rise.
8. Today's parents are less likely to believe that it is important to remain in an unhappy marriage for the sake of the children than they were 20 years ago.[3]

QUESTIONS:
1. Since you first met the Lord Jesus, what commitments have you made to Him? Which have you kept? Which have you dropped?
2. Why it is important for you to be commited to your local church?
3. Who is the most committed person in your chruch? What makes them stand out above others?

3. HE DID NOT QUIT NOR FORSAKE GOD (v.27).

It looked as if God had forsaken Epaphroditus. It seemed as though God had blessed him ever so richly until he had arrived in Rome. God had led the church in Philippi...

- to appoint him as a special messenger for the Lord and for the great Philippian church.
- to give him the coveted task of joining and ministering to the great evangelist and missionary Paul.

But when he arrived in Rome, he found out that by associating with Paul there was the danger of being judged as an insurrectionist—as a cohort of Paul. He was risking his own life by associating with Paul. And then, to top it off, he had become ill and almost died. God could have prevented it from happening. Why did He not stop it? A thousand questions flooded Epaphroditus' mind—each one tempting him to question and doubt God. He could have quit, forsaking the mission, and not too many people would have questioned his decision. In fact, the vast majority would have agreed, thinking it the course of wisdom.

But not Epaphroditus. He was not a quitter! He was not a coward! He was a true minister of God! God had done so much for him—especially in saving him and giving him the assurance of living forever—he could never quit nor forsake God.

ILLUSTRATION:

Often times, it is little children who come up with profound thoughts that few adults would dare share. Here is one such example:

The lawyer made it a regular habit to put his little girl to bed at night by reading her a Bible story. This particular night he read her the story of Job.

Her eyes lit up as she heard the story of the man who lost his wife, cattle, and children. His body was racked with sores and his friends forsook him. The little girl's summary of the events compelled her to ask her father this probing question:

"Daddy, why didn't Job sue God?"

APPLICATION:

God never promises a "rose garden," never promises life will be fair or easy. On the contrary, God plainly tells us to expect trials and problems throughout life. It is when we stand strong in the face of all these circumstances that our faith in God shines through, not when everything is running along smoothly.

We can curse God, blame God, abandon God, and, yes, even TRY to sue God—but a true Christian believer clings to God in time of trouble; he doesn't forsake God.

QUESTIONS:
1. Life appears to be unfair at times. What does God expect of you during these times?
2. How can you stand strong in the face of some great trial?
3. How can you strengthen your commitment to God?

4. CONCLUSION: THE APPEAL TO REJOICE AND TO RECEIVE THE PERSON WHO IS NOT A QUITTER (v.28-30).

Paul was sending Epaphroditus back to the church. In no sense of the word were they to question him because he was returning. He was returning because Paul was sending him back not because he was choosing to return. Therefore, the church was to joy in him and in his stedfast faithfulness.

Note the words "not regarding his life." A.T. Robertson points out that this is a gambling word, that it means to gamble one's life; to stake everything; to chance everything; to recklessly gamble. Epaphroditus staked his life for the ministry of Christ. He courageously risked his life.

APPLICATION:

Epaphroditus both challenges and rebukes a soft, easygoing Christianity and ministry. His life shows that Christianity is stern and demanding. It calls for self-denial and self-effacing sacrifice. It gives little thought to personal comfort and safety.

"**And he said to them all, If any man will come after me, let him deny himself, and take up his cross daily, and follow me. For whosoever will save his life shall lose it: but whosoever will lose his life for my sake, the same shall save it" (Lk.9:23-24).**

QUESTIONS:
1. Are you a risk-taker like Epaphroditus, a man who was willing to risk everything for the ministry of Christ?
2. What is the most courageous thing you have ever done? For whom did you do it? Would you do the same for a Christian brother or sister? For the church? For God?

PHILIPPIANS 2:25-30

SUMMARY:

We have seen the testimony of a man whose courage is an example for us to follow. Like Churchill, he never, never, never gave up. Like Epaphroditus...

1. We must learn to never quit nor forsake our Christian brothers and sisters in Christ.
2. We must learn to never quit nor forsake the church.
3. We must learn never to quit nor forsake God.
4. Result: If we never quit, then other believers will rejoice and receive us.

PERSONAL JOURNAL NOTES:
(Reflection & Response)

1. The most important thing that I learned from this lesson was:

2. The area that I need to work on the most is:

3. I can apply this lesson to my life by:

4. Closing Statement of Commitment:

[1]William Barclay, *The Letters to the Philippians, Colossians, and Thessalonians*, p.60f.
[2]William Barclay, *The Letters to the Philippians, Colossians, and Thessalonians*, p.61.
[3]George Barna, *The Frog In The Kettle* (Ventura,CA: Regal Books, 1990), p.34.
[4]A.T. Robertson, *Word Pictures in the New Testament*, Vol.4 Nashville, TN: Broadman Press, 1930), p.449.

PHILIPPIANS 3:1-3

	CHAPTER 3	write the same things to you, to me indeed is not grievous, but for you it is safe.	2. By heeding what is written (the Scripture)
	IV. THE "PRESS-ING ON" OF THE CHRIS-TIAN BE-LIEVER, 3:1-21	2 Beware of dogs, beware of evil work-ers, beware of the concision.	3. By watching out for false teachers
	A. Pressing On: Guarding Oneself, 3:1-3	3 For we are the cir-cumcision, which wor-ship God in the spirit, and rejoice in Christ	4. By knowing that you are the true (spiritual) circumci-sion, a true believer
1. By rejoicing in the Lord	Finally, my brethren, rejoice in the Lord. To	Jesus, and have no confidence in the flesh.	

Section IV
THE "PRESSING ON" OF THE CHRISTIAN BELIEVER,
Philippians 3:1-21

Study 1:   PRESSING ON—GUARDING ONESELF

Text: Philippians 3:1-3

Aim: To learn how to constantly guard your Christian life.

Memory Verse:
"For we are the circumcision [true believers], which worship God in the spirit, and rejoice in Christ Jesus, and have no confidence in the flesh" (Philippians 3:3).

INTRODUCTION:
You can take almost any scenario in life—cleaning house, building a house, raising kids, working at a job—and understand that each area needs maintenance. It is not enough just to do something once and expect that it will forever keep working, stay fixed, stay clean, or take care of itself. Everything and everyone needs to be nurtured to keep on track. The same is true with our Christian faith.

It is a terrible misconception to believe that personal growth for a Christian believer is natural and easy. Pressing on in our faith requires hard work and effort. Paul tells us in chapter three how to go about pressing on.

This chapter is one of the great chapters of the Bible, a chapter that needs to be studied time and again. It includes the great personal testimony and ambition of Paul. It gives us some of the great principles that governed Paul's life. The subject of the chapter is "The Pressing On Of The Christian Believer." These are some things the Christian believer must do as he presses on for Christ. First, he must guard himself.

OUTLINE:
1.   By rejoicing in the Lord (v.1).
2.   By heeding what is written (the Scripture) (v.1).
3.   By watching out for false teachers (v.2).
4.   By knowing that you are the true (spiritual) circumcision, a true believer (v.3).

86

1. BY REJOICING IN THE LORD (v.1).

A person who is always rejoicing in the Lord will not go astray. As the believer walks through life, two things are always confronting him: bad or unfortunate circumstances and false teaching. No matter where he goes, the trials of life, both minor and major, confront him. He has to stand face to face with the awful trials of life including...

- enticing temptations
- lust of the eyes
- lust of the flesh
- greed
- selfishness
- arguments

- division
- inhuman behavior
- criminal acts
- death
- accidents
- disease

The list could go on and on. Note another fact as well. No matter where he walks, the false teachings of this life confront him. No matter which way the believer turns, he is confronted with different ideas about how to handle life and its great trials.

⇒ There is the teaching that says, "Eat, drink, and be merry, for tomorrow we die. Ignore the trials and problems of life."
⇒ There is the teaching that says, "Discipline and control yourself. Take care of your body and mind." But it ignores the spiritual.
⇒ There is the teaching that says, "Don't go overboard. Enjoy life—join in—do what you want; but do it within reason."
⇒ There is the teaching that says religion is the answer to both life and death, "Join a religious body, undergo its rituals, adopt its beliefs, and live the best you can. God will accept you."

The list of false teachings could go on and on. The point is this: the believer is bombarded by both trials and false teachings every day of his life. Therefore, he must guard himself, and the first guard is to rejoice in the Lord. If he walks throughout the day rejoicing in the Lord, his mind is upon the Lord. He rejoices over what Christ has done for him—rejoices over the Lord's...

- justifying him
- adopting him
- reconciling him
- saving him
- loving him
- delivering him
- guiding and directing him
- securing righteousness for him

- dying for him—bearing his sin and condemnation
- arising for him—giving him a new life
- looking after him
- giving him the privilege of knowing God
- giving him victory over sin
- giving him hope of eternal life

Now note, the great thing that rejoicing does is this: *it places and keeps a person in the presence of Christ.* No matter what confronts the believer—no matter how terrible the trial—he knows that he is being looked after by Christ. He knows that nothing can separate him from the Lord and His love—that he shall never die but rather live eternally. Therefore, he knows that whatever comes upon him can never conquer and overcome him. Christ will give him supernatural power and strength to overcome it. And if he is called upon to lay down his body and move on to heaven, he knows that he shall never taste or experience death; he knows that Christ is going to escort him right on into God's presence immediately—quicker than the eye can blink—about 11/100 of a second. The believer is forever secure in the keeping power of the Lord Jesus Christ. Therefore, he walks rejoicing in the Lord: he rejoices no matter what confronts him.

APPLICATION:

When a person rejoices in the Lord, his mind is focused upon the Lord, upon what the Lord has done for him. And *the mind cannot be two places at once.* If it is upon the Lord and His glorious salvation, then it cannot be upon the trials and false teachings of this world.

"But let all those that put their trust in thee rejoice: let them ever shout for joy, because thou defendest them: let them also that love thy name be joyful in thee" (Ps.5:11).

ILLUSTRATION:

Rejoicing in the Lord gives the Christian believer a different perspective of life than what the world offers, for example:

"A Coloradan moved to Texas and built a house with a large picture window from which he could view hundreds of miles of rangeland. 'The only problem is,' he said, 'there's nothing to see.'
"About the same time, a Texan moved to Colorado and built a house with a large picture window overlooking the Rockies. 'The only problem is I can't see anything,' he said. 'The mountains are in the way.'"[1]

Rejoicing in the Lord will bring contentment—no matter where you are or what is happening to you.

QUESTIONS:
1. Is it possible to rejoice in the Lord when things are going badly?
2. Why should you walk throughout the day rejoicing in the Lord?
3. What are some things you have to rejoice over?

2. BY HEEDING WHAT IS WRITTEN (THE SCRIPTURE) (v.1).

Note: Paul says that he is writing some things that he had apparently written before. What he is about to write is so important that it has to be repeated. The church must do what is being said.

The point is this: the writings of Paul and of Scripture must be heeded. To heed means to guard, to pay attention to. What Scripture says was written to instruct us and to help us in *pressing on* for Christ. No person can press on apart from heeding the Scriptures. If he fails to study and obey the Scripture, he will cave in either to the trials of life or to false teaching. Only as we obey the Scripture—the commandments of the Lord—can we show our love and loyalty to the Lord Jesus Christ.

"Study to show thyself approved unto God, a workman that needeth not to be ashamed, rightly dividing the word of truth" (2 Tim.2:15).

ILLUSTRATION:

Have you ever tried to bargain with God...
- By trying to find loop-holes?
- By obeying Him in the "easy" things?
- By passing up His hard instructions?
- By highlighting the "juicy" promises of the Bible and overlooking the hard sayings that require tough decisions?

Doctor Charles Stanley of Atlanta, GA, has said in his teaching that *obedience* to God is defined as *"Doing:*
⇒ *what He says*
⇒ *when He says*
⇒ *how He says*
⇒ *all He says*
Anything less than this is not obedience, but disobedience."

The Christian who wants to press on must obey the Scriptures in all points. Anything less than obedience is disobedience.

3. BY WATCHING OUT FOR FALSE TEACHERS (v.2).

Paul was always facing false teachers who were savage in their attacks upon him. He mentions three groups of false teachers in this verse.

1.   *Beware of false teachers who act like dogs.* It should be noted that both Jew and Gentile called each other dogs as a term of contempt. The word "dogs" was the lowest title possible to convey contempt and ridicule. Dog does not refer to the house pet of today, but to the wild dogs that roamed in the forests by day and the city streets by night. They were scavengers and snarlers who could be very vicious and dangerous.

The point is descriptive: there are some false teachers who are just like wild dogs.
⇒   They are scavengers who seek out all whom they can consume with their false teaching. And if any believer steps forward to defend the sheep and the truth, they snarl, often becoming vicious and dangerous, ready to attack the defender and destroy him.

> **"Beware of false prophets, which come to you in sheep's clothing,**
> **but inwardly they are ravening wolves" (Mt.7:15).**

2.   *Beware of false teachers who are evil workers.* The world is full of people who work evil things.
⇒   This refers to those who hold to and teach high standards of righteousness, morality, and religion. They are absolutely sure they are righteous and good—at least good enough to be acceptable to God. They think there is just no way God would ever reject them.
⇒   This also refers to those who teach evil by the way they live and talk about morality, righteousness and religion. Some live base, immoral, indulgent, and extravagant lives, while others try to mix both a religious and indulgent life-style together.

The point is this: there are those who are always opposing the Lord Jesus Christ and His salvation by grace alone. They do not accept that Christ is God's Son—that He is the Lord of man's life. Therefore, they accept His teaching but ignore or deny salvation by His blood. They stand opposed to the gospel of salvation by His grace alone. They go about establishing their own way to God, doing whatever good they feel is needed to make themselves acceptable to Him. The result is false teaching—a way to God that stands against the Lord Jesus Christ and His way. Such false teachers are evil workers—workers who stand opposed to the truth.

3.   *Beware of false teachers who are of the concision.* The concision refers to the Judaizers, the legalists, or religionists who *refuse to accept salvation by grace alone.* These teachers stress the 'other' things (traditions, rituals, ceremonies, etc.) that have to be done to be saved. They erase the value of Christ's death on the cross by 'adding to it' other things necessary to receive salvation.

> **"For they being ignorant of God's righteousness, and going about to**
> **establish their own righteousness, have not submitted themselves unto the**
> **righteousness of God. For Christ is the end of the law for righteousness to**
> **every one that believeth. For Moses describeth the righteousness which is**
> **of the law, That the man which doeth those things shall live by them"**
> **(Ro.10:3-5).**

ILLUSTRATION:
Note that this verse begins with a striking warning: *"Beware of dogs"* (v.2). J. Vernon McGee gives an excellent illustration on this point.

"This is not a word of warning to the mailmen. I once had a dog that hated mail-men, and I don't know why. We changed mailmen several times during the period we had him, and he had the same attitude toward each of them. But Paul is not referring to animals in this verse. We will get some insight into his thinking by turning back to the prophecy of Isaiah who warned against the false prophets of his day: 'His watchmen are blind: they are all ignorant, they are all dumb dogs, they cannot bark; sleeping, ly-ing down, loving to slumber' [Isa.56:10]. Isaiah was warning the people against the false prophets who were attempting to comfort the people and were telling them that everything was find instead of warning them of coming disaster....

"In Isaiah's day there were a great many false prophets who were comforting the people when they should have been warning them. Isaiah likens the false prophets to dumb dogs. You see, a good sheep dog is constantly alert to danger. If a lion or a bear makes a foray into the flock, that dog will bark like mad and run it away if he can. He gives warning of the approach of any kind of danger. But the false prophets gave no warning at all. Therefore the southern kingdom had been lulled to sleep and resented Isaiah's effort to arouse them.

" America today is in the same position. We are going to sleep, my friend, under the comfortable blanket of affluence. We like the idea of comfort, of getting something for nothing, of taking it easy, of having a good day. My feeling is that somebody ought to do a little barking.

"So Paul warned, 'Beware of dogs'—beware of men who are constantly comforting you and are not giving you the Word of God."

APPLICATION:

It is disturbing, but true, that the major recruiting grounds for cults are in the Protestant churches in America. This is because so many just do not know the basic truths of the faith.

QUESTIONS:
1. Why is it important for you to know what and why you believe?
2. What are some basic doctrines that make Christianity distinctive from other religions or cults?

4. BY KNOWING THAT YOU ARE THE TRUE [SPIRITUAL] CIRCUMCISION, A TRUE BELIEVER (v.3).

Note that believers are called *the circumcision*. What does Paul mean?
1.   Believers are those who worship God as He really wishes to be worshipped: in the spirit; that is, they have circumcised or cut away the flesh as the means by which they worship God. Think for a moment: How do most people attempt to worship God?
⇒ by attending church services
⇒ by praying
⇒ by making occasional gifts to needy causes
⇒ by thinking of God occasionally
⇒ by being circumcised or baptized or undergoing some other ritual
⇒ by keeping the rituals and ceremonies of a church
⇒ by joining a church
⇒ by observing special days

But note a critical point: as good as all of these are, they are not the basis of true worship. They are things that we do *because* we worship; they are the result and activities of worship. True, they may help us to focus upon God, stirring us to worship Him, but the basis of worship is the Spirit of God.

To worship God, man must have the Spirit of God living within him. He no longer worships God externally through rituals and ceremonies. He now worships God inwardly through the Spirit of God who lives within him.

> "The true worshippers shall worship the Father in spirit and in truth: for the Father seeketh such to worship him. God is a Spirit: and they that worship him must worship him in spirit and in truth" (Jn.4:23-24).

2. Believers are those who rejoice as God really wants us to rejoice: in Christ Jesus. Christ Jesus...
- is God's only begotten Son.
- is the Person who gave Himself to die for us, bearing our sins and condemnation.
- is the Person who has saved us, made it possible for us to live forever in the presence of God.
- is the only Savior, the only acceptable way to enter God's presence.

Therefore, it is only natural that God expects us to rejoice in Christ Jesus. How could we boast and rejoice in ritual and ceremony and religion? The Source—the Author and Finisher—of our faith is Christ Jesus. Therefore, the true circumcision, the true believer does not boast in anything physical or material—not in ritual or ceremony or religion. The true circumcision—the true believer—rejoices and boasts in Him who has given us salvation and access to God: Christ Jesus our Lord.

> "Rejoice in the Lord always: and again I say, Rejoice" (Ph.4:4).

3. Believers are those who have no confidence in the flesh. The flesh...
- is only physical and material.
- can only handle physical and material things.
- can only do good works and keep external rituals and ceremonies and religious practices.
- can do nothing beyond the physical and material.
- cannot penetrate the spiritual world or dimension of being.

The flesh ages, deteriorates, and corrupts. Therefore, the flesh goes the way of all material and physical substances: it dies and decays. And no matter what the flesh has done and accomplished in this physical world, it takes all its works to the grave with it. Therefore, the true circumcision, the true believer, has no confidence and puts no stock in the flesh. He has confidence only in Jesus Christ.

> "For he that soweth to his flesh shall of the flesh reap corruption; but he that soweth to the Spirit shall of the Spirit reap life everlasting" (Gal.6:8).

APPLICATION:

True worship has to be of the heart and spirit. Why? Because a man can attend church, keep all the rituals and ceremonies, and still be living in the depths of sin. But if a man's spirit is right with God, he worships God with a clean and pure heart, free from all sin and defilement. The truly circumcised person is the person who worships God in spirit.

> "What? know ye not that your body is the temple of the Holy Ghost which is in you, which ye have of God, and ye are not your own? For ye are bought with a price: therefore glorify God in your body, and in your spirit, which are God's" (1 Cor.6:19-20).

QUESTIONS:
1. What are the ways in which you regularly worship God? Where? When? Why? How?
2. Do you ever just go through the motions without really worshipping God in your heart?
3. What does it mean to worship God in the spirit? What can you do to develop your worship so that it is truly pleasing to the Father?

A CLOSER LOOK:

Before Christ, circumcision was the physical sign that a man was a follower of the true God. It was the sign that a man believed the promises that God had made to Abraham and Israel (cp. Gen. 17:10-14; Ro.4:11). God never intended circumcision to have any value other than being a sign. It was not to bring righteousness to any man—not even to Abraham (Ro.4:9-10). It was given only as a sign—a sign of the faith that a man already had in God's promises. Righteousness was credited to the man because he believed God's promises; then the man was circumcised as a sign of his faith in God

However, many abused God's purpose for circumcision.

1. Some made circumcision a substitute for true righteousness. A man was thought to be safe and secure in the arms of God if he was circumcised. Believing God and loving men had little to do with being a child of God. Many forgot the circumcision of a pure heart and became Jews of the circumcision in name only. Circumcision became merely an external and physical sign.

2. Some used circumcision as a way to divide and categorize people. A great wall of division was thrown up around the uncircumcised (cp. Acts 10:1; 1 Sam.17:26, 36; 2 Sam.1:20). Any man who was uncircumcised was thought to be *cut off* and *far off*, not only from those thought to be the people of God (the Jews and the circumcised) but from God Himself. An uncircumcised man was looked upon with bitter contempt. In the mind of the Jew, God was thought to love only Israel, despising and rejecting all other people (the Gentile nations).

3. God has done away with circumcision as a sign of righteousness since Christ has come (Gal.5:6; 6:15; Col.2:11). Righteousness is now of the heart, in the spirit, and not in the letter of rules and regulations (cp. Ro.2:25-29; 4:8-12, 23-25). The truly righteous man is the man who is God's *inwardly*—the man whose spirit has been *re-created* into the very nature of God. God's very own righteous nature is implanted into the very nature of man when he is *born again*. A man *born again* by the Spirit of God is God's "new creation" (Jn.3:3f; 1 Pt.1:20; 2 Pt.1:4).

SUMMARY:

We press on and guard ourselves by:

1. Rejoicing in the Lord, staying in His presence always.
2. Heeding what is written in Scripture and being obedient.
3. Watching out for false teachers.
4. Knowing that we are the true circumcision, the true believers.

PERSONAL JOURNAL NOTES:
(Reflection & Response)

1. The most important thing that I learned from this lesson was:

2. The area that I need to work on the most is:

3. I can apply this lesson to my life by:

4. Closing Statement of Commitment:

[1]Craig B. Larson, Editor, *Illustrations for Preaching and Teaching*, p.241.
[2]J. Vernon McGee, *Thru The Bible* Vol.5 (Nashville, TN: Thomas Nelson Publishers, 1983), p.311.

	B. Pressing on: Paul's Personal Testimony-- Rejecting Self-righteousness & Seeking Perfection, 3:4-16	faith: Christ, the righteousness which is of God	
		10 That I may know him, and the power of his resurrection, and the fellowship of his sufferings, being made conformable unto his death;	d. Paul sought a victorious experience with Christ: To know His glorious power over the world & over all that is in the world
1. Paul had achieved the height of self-righteousness, but he rejected it	4 Though I might also have confidence in the flesh. If any other man thinketh that he hath whereof he might trust in the flesh, I more:	11 If by any means I might attain unto the resurrection of the dead.	e. Paul sought an eternal experience with Christ: To be resurrected from the dead
a. He had the right parents	5 Circumcised the eighth day, of the stock of Israel, of the tribe of Benjamin, an Hebrew of the Hebrews; as touching the law, a Pharisee;	12 Not as though I had already attained, either were already perfect: but I follow after, if that I may apprehend that for which also I am apprehended of Christ Jesus.	3. Paul did not count himself as having yet arrived--he was not yet perfect
b. He had the heritage			a. He followed after his God-given purpose
c. He had the social status			
d. He had the faithfulness			
e. He had the religion	6 Concerning zeal, persecuting the church; touching the righteousness which is in the law, blameless.	13 Brethren, I count not myself to have apprehended: but this one thing I do, forgetting those things which are behind, and reaching forth unto those things which are before,	b. He worked at forgetting the past
f. He had the religious zeal			
g. He had the morality			
2. Paul sought to win Christ--His righteousness, His perfection	7 But what things were gain to me, those I counted loss for Christ.		
a. Paul had a past experience with Christ: He had counted his own righteousness as loss	8 Yea doubtless, and I count all things but loss for the excellency of the knowledge of Christ Jesus my Lord: for whom I have suffered the loss of all things, and do count them but dung, that I may win Christ,	14 I press toward the mark for the prize of the high calling of God in Christ Jesus.	c. He pressed on toward the goal, toward God's purpose in Christ Jesus
b. Paul had a continuous experience with Christ: He counted all things as waste		15 Let us therefore, as many as be perfect, be thus minded: and if in any thing ye be otherwise minded, God shall reveal even this unto you.	d. He kept his mind on growing, on maturing in Christ
c. Paul sought a future exerience with Christ: to be found in Christ	9 And be found in him, not having mine own righteousness, which is of the law, but that which is through the faith of by	16 Nevertheless, whereto we have already attained, let us walk by the same rule, let us mind the same thing.	e. He maintained the growth he had already achieved

Section IV
THE 'PRESSING ON' OF THE CHRISTIAN BELIEVER,
Philippians 3:1-21

(Note: Because of the length of this outline and commentary, you may wish to split this passage into two or three studies.)

PHILIPPIANS 3:4-16

Study 2: **PRESSING ON: PAUL'S PERSONAL TESTIMONY—REJECTING SELF-RIGHTEOUSNESS & SEEKING PERFECTION**

Text: **Philippians 3:4-16**

Aim: To reject self-righteousness and pursue the righteousness of Christ.

Memory Verse:
> "I press toward the mark for the prize of the high calling of God in Christ Jesus" (Philippians 3:14).

INTRODUCTION

All across the world men sense they need a relationship with God. But some men are never sure whether or not things are right with God. They lack perfect assurance and confidence that they please God enough to be acceptable to Him. They have a hope that God will accept them, but they do not know, not with absolute certainty.

It is these feelings that have stirred the religions of the world. Men want to be right with God; they want to be approved and accepted by God. They want God to look after them and help them, and they want God to accept them when this life is over. Therefore, they set out to do what they feel will make them *good enough* to be acceptable to God. They try to do whatever good they feel is necessary to please *their god*. Granted, the degree to which men feel this differs among all men. One man will feel that he has to be extremely good, whereas another man feels that he has to be moderately good. The point to note is this: *this kind of religion* is a religion...

- of works
- of doing good
- of being good
- of making oneself acceptable to God
- of securing God's favor
- of making oneself approved by God

It is a religion of self-righteousness—of becoming as righteous and good as a person can—of earning and meriting God's favor—of working one's way into God's presence. There is, of course, a severe fallacy with this approach to God.

God is perfect, but not a single person is perfect. No person can do enough good to become perfect no matter what he does. In fact, man is already imperfect; and once perfection is lost, it is lost.

The point is this: no person can ever earn or merit the right to live in God's presence. If a person is ever going to live in God's presence, it will be because God loves the person enough to accept him and to transform him into a perfect person. This is exactly what God does through Jesus Christ. God accepts men *through His Son*, through the love and grace of His Son.

It was this, the gospel of Jesus Christ, that Paul had missed before his conversion. And it is this that so many in the world miss. Paul had never seen the great love of God for man. Yet, *above all men*, he had given his life to seeking after God, doing all the good he could to make himself acceptable to God. But despite all his achievements, he still did not have peace with God. Perfect assurance and confidence of living eternally with God was still lacking. This is the message of the present passage: Paul's personal testimony—his rejection of self-righteousness and turning to the righteousness of Jesus Christ.

OUTLINE:
1. Paul had achieved the height of self-righteousness, but he rejected it (v.4-6).
2. Paul sought to win Christ—His righteousness and perfection (v.7-11).
3. Paul did not count himself as having yet arrived—he was not yet perfect (v.12-16).

PHILIPPIANS 3:4-16

1. PAUL HAD ACHIEVED THE HEIGHT OF SELF-RIGHTEOUSNESS, BUT HE REJECTED IT (v.4-6).

Paul ranks among the greatest of men who have attempted to work their way into God's presence. Paul did all the good he could to secure God's approval. Few if any men have ever attained what Paul did by human effort. Yet, it was all to no avail. His goodness and his attainments did not make him acceptable to God. And there is one primary reason: he could not make himself perfect.

However, note what Paul says: "If any man thinks he can trust in the works and attainments of his flesh, I more. I can trust and boast in the goodness and morality and works of the flesh as much as any man who has ever lived." This is a phenomenal claim, but Paul lists seven privileges and achievements which show the total inadequacy of man to save himself. Paul divided the list under "Privileges of Birth" and "Achievements by Self-Effort."

1.   The privileges of birth are three in particular.
    a.   "Circumcised the eighth day" (v.5): Paul was saying that he had the *right birth*. A true Jewish family always had its male child circumcised when he was just eight days old. Circumcision was the sign that a person believed in God and in His promises—in particular the promise that the Jews were the promised and covenant people of God. Paul was claiming to be a true Jewish believer who had the privilege of believing parents.

APPLICATION:
Paul was saying that goodness and righteousness are not found in birth nor in religious rituals and ceremonies. Yet, how many people think they are acceptable to God because they...
    •   have godly parents?
    •   have a godly spouse?
    •   have godly children?
    •   have godly friends?
    •   have kept religious rituals and ceremonies?
How many expect the godliness of others to rub off on them—to count for them and to make them acceptable to God?

QUESTION:
1.   What makes people think that the godliness of others will rub off on them? That God will accept them because they have godly parents, spouses, etc.?

    b.   "Of the stock of Israel" (v.5): Paul was saying that he had the *right national heritage* and a very special relationship with God. He was born in the right nation, among the right people. The name *Israel* goes back to the time when God changed Jacob's name to Israel. Jacob had a special need, and God met his need in a very special way through a dream and changed his name (Gen.32:28). When a Jew wished to stress his special relationship to God, he called himself an Israelite; that is, he was of the nation and descent of Israel which had a very special relationship with God and who had received a very special name from God.

APPLICATION:
Paul was saying that goodness and righteousness are not found in ancestors nor in social superiority. Yet, how many think that being born in a Christian nation and surrounded by Christian principles carry some merit with God? How many feel that the people of a so called Christian nation are more acceptable to God than the heathen of some idol-worshipping tribe in the depths of a jungle? How many feel that they have some merit with God because they have a Christian name? How many feel they have a little better relationship with God and are a little more acceptable to God because they live in a so called religious nation?

96

c. "Of the tribe of Benjamin" (v.5): Benjamin was considered the aristocratic tribe of Israel because of the tribe's loyalty when so many other tribes were disloyal (1 Ki.12:1) and because of the tribe's courageous acts throughout Israel's history (Judg.5:14; Hos.5:8). Paul was saying that he was of the *highest aristocracy, of the most noble, of the most respectable persons of Israel.*

APPLICATION:

Paul was saying that goodness and righteousness are not found in social or religious status. Yet, how many feel they are *more acceptable* to God because they belong to...

- an upper class?
- a more elite church?
- a more dynamic church?
- a more active ministry?

2. The achievements by self-effort are four in number.
   a. "An Hebrew of the Hebrews" (v.5): Paul claimed to have the *right language* and the *right customs.* When the Jews were conquered and scattered over the world, a believing Jew refused to give up his Jewish language and customs. He continued using Hebrew and he continued to practice Jewish customs. Every Jew did not, but Paul says he and his family did. What Paul meant was that he had *the mark of faithfulness.* He had deliberately kept the Hebrew tongue and refused to forget it. In his day, this was extremely difficult, for the Jews were literally scattered across the world and the world had one common language, Greek. But Paul remained stedfast. He learned and refused to forget the right language. He was loyal to the elect race of God. He was untinged by other philosophies.

APPLICATION:

Paul was saying that goodness and righteousness are not found in religious faithfulness, nor in a spiritual language, nor in the ability to know and speak in religious terms. Yet, how many think that they are acceptable to God because they...

- do good and are faithful in being good?
- are faithful in studying their religion, the Bible, and the great doctrines of the faith?
- are faithful in talking about and sharing spiritual things?
- know and use religious terms and languages?

   b. "A Pharisee" (v.5): Paul claimed to have had the *right religion*; to have been a Pharisee. The Pharisees were strict religionists, so strict their very name meant *The Separated Ones.* Paul said that he was of the strictest religious sect ever known. He devoted his whole life to the most *separated* and demanding religion ever known to man. He achieved *separation,* an exacting separation from other men.

APPLICATION:

Paul was saying that goodness and righteousness are not found in religion, not even in being a follower of the true religion. Yet, how many feel the very opposite?

ILLUSTRATION:

Dr. J. Vernon McGee says:

"I remember hearing Dr. Carroll say, 'When I was converted, I lost my religion.' A great many people need to lose their religion and find Jesus Christ as Paul did. He was so revolutionized that what had been his prized possession is now relegated to the garbage can!"[1]

c. "Zeal" (v.6): Paul had zealously stood and fought for his religion. He hotly pursued and persecuted the church. Paul had such a zeal for his religion that he sought to wipe out any cause that differed from his (Acts 22:2-21; 26:4-33; 1 Cor.15:8-10; Gal.1:13).

APPLICATION:

Paul was saying that goodness and righteousness are not found in religious commitment or zeal. Few have ever been committed to their religion like Paul—few have ever been as faithful to the worship services, ordinances, rituals, and ceremonies of his religion as Paul. Paul was a religionist among religionists. Few have ever proclaimed and protected their religion like Paul. Paul was as zealous as a person could be in trying to reach converts for his religion and in keeping his religion as pure as he could.

d. "Blameless" (v.6): Paul claimed he had sought to keep the law and he had kept it—completely and fully. This does not mean that Paul was sinless; it means that when Paul sinned, he obeyed the law and took his sacrifice to the temple. He obeyed all the commandments, rituals, and ceremonies just like Scripture said. He followed all the laws and instructions of the Scripture. He was blameless—ritually and ceremonially—in the righteousness of the law.

APPLICATION:

Paul was saying that goodness and righteousness are not found in keeping all the rituals and ceremonies of religion. They are not even found in keeping all the commandments of the Scripture.

"For I say unto you, That except your righteousness shall
exceed the righteousness of the scribes and Pharisees, ye shall
in no case enter into the kingdom of heaven" (Mt.5:20).

QUESTIONS:
1. Have you ever felt that your heritage—your parents, grandparents, church, pastor, friends, etc.—were going to be influential in your gaining eternal life, in receiving the righteousness of Christ?
2. Have you ever felt that you were good enough to achieve righteousness on your own?
3. Have you ever felt that you were so bad that there was no hope of receiving the righteousness of Christ?
4. If your answer was yes to any of the above questions, do you still feel that way now? Why?
5. What are some ways that men attempt to be righteous?

2. PAUL SOUGHT TO WIN CHRIST—HIS RIGHTEOUSNES, HIS PERFECTION (v.7-11).

The one thing in life that Paul sought was the righteousness and perfection of Jesus Christ. He knew that no matter how good he became, he could never become perfect. He still came short and he was still doomed to face death. Therefore, his only hope of living forever was focusing his heart and life upon Jesus Christ, trusting the righteousness and perfection of Jesus Christ to *cover him.* He lived for Jesus Christ, and he trusted God to honor his commitment. If God did not do this, he was lost and doomed to death forever, for he could never gain perfection on his own. His only hope was Christ. This is what the present passage is all about. Paul believed this glorious fact: if he trusted Jesus Christ—if he sought after the righteousness and perfection of Jesus Christ with all that he was and had—God would take his faith and *count it as righteousness.* God would honor his commitment to His Son by accepting and giving him eternal life. Note five significant points.

1.   Paul had a *past experience* with Christ: there was a time when he had counted *his own righteousness* as loss (v.7). Paul was referring to his conversion experience. There was a time when he had given up his own self-righteousness and works, his own attempts to become perfect.

    a.   Note that this is a past experience, a once-for-all experience. It is a definite time when Paul made a decision to follow Christ. If Paul was to become righteous and perfect, he had to trust the love of God to cover him with the righteousness and perfection of Christ.

    b.   Note also that this did not mean that Paul quit trying to live for God. On the contrary, it meant that Paul tried more diligently than ever to live for God. When God saw Paul's total commitment to Christ, He knew that Paul's faith was genuine. God knew that Paul really believed that Christ was his Savior, that Christ was his hope for perfection and righteousness—for eternity.

APPLICATION:

    God sees our faith; whether or not it is genuine. Genuine faith makes a total commitment to Jesus Christ. A person who truly believes in Jesus Christ gives all he is and has to Christ. He counts his own effort and works, his own righteousness as loss—as nothing—in order to gain Christ.

    "But without faith it is impossible to please him: for he that cometh to God must believe that he is, and that he is a rewarder of them that diligently <u>seek him</u>" (Heb.11:6).

QUESTIONS:
1.   Have you...
    a.   recognized and accepted that you can never achieve righteousness on your own?
    b.   rejected and denied yourself—your own self-righteousness—and began to seek after Christ and His righteousness?
    c.   trusted the righteousness of Christ to save you?
2.   Would you share your salvation experience with Christ with others?

2.   Paul had a *continuous experience* with Christ: he constantly counted all things as loss and as waste in order to win Christ (v.8). The word "count" is in the present tense; it is continuous action. When a person has made the decision to seek after Christ, he is *to continue* to seek after the knowledge of Christ—to learn all he can about the righteousness and perfection of Jesus Christ.

    a.   Note that the knowledge of Christ is said to be excellent: it is the excellency of the knowledge of Christ Jesus our Lord. The knowledge of Jesus Christ is the most excellent knowledge in all the world. No other knowledge can give a person righteousness and perfection. No other knowledge can make a person acceptable to God and give him the right to live eternally.

    b.   Note what Paul says: "I have suffered the loss of all things." The phrase *all things* includes not only the religious position Paul had attained, but all the other areas of his life as well. The Greek scholar Kenneth Wuest gives a graphic description of what Paul gave up to become a Christian believer.

    "Paul was a citizen of Tarsus. At the time he lived there, only families of wealth and reputation were allowed to retain their Tarsian citizenship. This throws a flood of light upon Paul's early life. He was born into a home of wealth and culture. His family were wealthy Jews living in one of the most progressive of oriental cities. All this Paul left to become a poor itinerant missionary.

    "But not only did he forfeit all this when he was saved, but his parents would have nothing to do with a son who had in their estimation dishonored them by becoming one of those hated, despised Christians. They had reared

him in the lap of luxury, had sent him to the Jewish school of theology in Jerusalem to sit at the feet of the great Gamaliel, and had given him an excellent training in Greek culture at the University of Tarsus, a Greek school of learning. But they had now cast him off. He was still forfeiting all that he had held dear, what for? He tells us, 'that I may win Christ.'"²

"Then Peter began to say unto him, Lo, we have left all, and have followed thee" (Mk.10:28).

<u>QUESTIONS:</u>
1. What kinds of things did you give up to win (follow) Christ?
2. Are you continuing to live a sacrificial life, to give up things in order to win and follow after Christ?
3. What do you need to give up in order to be assured—absolutely assured—that you will win Christ and be counted righteous?

3. Paul sought a *future experience* with Christ: he sought to be found in Christ (v.9). Paul was looking ahead either to death or to the return of Christ. When he came face to face with God, he wanted to be *found in Christ*. He wanted to stand before God in the righteousness of Jesus Christ, not in his own righteousness.

"Christ, the righteousness which is of God" (v.9).

<u>ILLUSTRATION:</u>
"This is the verse that came to John Bunyan as he walked through the cornfields one night, wondering how he could stand before God. He said that suddenly he saw himself—not just as a sinner, but as sin from the crown of his head to the soles of his feet. He realized that he had nothing, and that Christ had everything."³

4. Paul sought a *victorious experience* with Christ: he sought to know Christ—to know His glorious power over the world and all that is in the world (v.10). This is one of the Bible's great verses of Scripture, a verse that should be memorized and that should dominate the believer's life. As clearly seen throughout this whole passage, Paul's great pursuit in life was to know Christ. This verse spells out exactly what he meant by knowing Christ.
   a. To know Christ is to know the power of His resurrection (v.10). The power of the Lord's resurrection refers to three great things
      ⇒ The power to raise Christ shows that God has the power to conquer all the trials and temptations of life, even the most powerful—death.
      ⇒ The resurrection of Jesus Christ shows that God has the power to give man a new life.
      ⇒ The power to raise Christ from the dead shows that God has the power to raise men from the dead.
   b. To know Christ is to know the fellowship of His sufferings (v.10). Most of us are willing to share in the blessings of Christ but we want nothing to do with the sufferings of Christ. We shrink from the ridicule, questioning, and abuse He had to bear. There is nothing pleasant about suffering pain and having people oppose us. There is nothing wrong with being honest about the fact. Paul said that he wanted to know the *fellowship* of the Lord's sufferings. That is, he wanted to share in *the purpose for which Christ was suffering*. Why did Christ suffer? He suffered because He proclaimed the righteousness and salvation of God—because He proclaimed the way men could become acceptable to God and live forever. Paul was saying that he wanted to suffer right along with Christ, suffer for the same cause—suffer for proclaiming the righteousness and salvation of God.
      There is no question about it: if we live for Christ—proclaim the righteousness and salvation of God—we shall suffer persecution. Why? Why would the world persecute anyone who brings the hope of eternal life to them? Because some persons want to live their lives like they want, and a righteous life and message con-

demns them. Therefore, they oppose anything that keeps them from living a life that pleases their own personal desires and flesh. The believer must know: he shall suffer persecution if he truly follows Christ.

> **"Yea, and all that will live godly in Christ Jesus shall suffer persecution" (2 Tim.3:12).**

Note one other thing: God draws close to the believer when he suffers for the cause of Christ. God gives a very special sense of His presence, love, and care when the believer is suffering. In fact, His presence is so near and dear it is called "the spirit of glory and of God" which rests upon the suffering believer.

> **"If ye be reproached for the name of Christ, happy are ye;**
> **for the spirit of glory and of God resteth upon you: on their part**
> **he is evil spoken of, but on your part he is glorified" (1 Pt.4:14).**

c. To know Christ is to be made conformable to His death (v.10). Jesus Christ subjected Himself totally to God. He put His own flesh and desires to death; He did only what God willed and desired. Even when He died, His flesh did not desire to die. He did not want to take the sins of the world upon Himself and be separated from God (cp. Mt.26:39, 42). But He subjected Himself to God's will. God willed Him to die for the sins of the world; therefore, Christ subjected His flesh and desires to do exactly what God willed. He subjected His flesh and desires and died for the sins of men.

Paul sought to be conformed to the death of Christ. He sought to subject himself totally to God—to put his flesh and desires to death and to do only the will and desire of God.

⇒ Paul sought to *deny himself and take up the cross* of Christ daily.

> **"And he said to them all, If any man will come after me, let him deny himself, and take up his cross daily, and follow me" (Lk.9:23).**

⇒ Paul sought to *crucify his old man* with Christ.

> **"Knowing this, that our old man is crucified with him, that the body of sin might be destroyed, that henceforth we should not serve sin" (Ro.6:6).**

⇒ Paul sought to *count himself dead* to sin but alive to God.
> **"Likewise reckon ye also yourselves to be dead indeed unto sin, but alive unto God through Jesus Christ our Lord" (Ro.6:11).**

⇒ Paul sought to be *crucified with Christ*.

> **"I am crucified with Christ: nevertheless I live; yet not I, but Christ liveth in me: and the life which I now live in the flesh I live by the faith of the Son of God, who loved me, and gave himself for me" (Gal.2:20).**

QUESTIONS:
1. Have you taken the steps that Paul took to have a victorious experience with Christ...
   ...denied yourself and taken up the cross of Christ daily?
   ...crucified your old nature with Christ?
   ...counted yourself dead to sin but alive to God?
   ...crucified yourself with Christ?

2. What do you think it means "to know the power of His resurrection"?
3. We are to also know Christ in His sufferings. This is a seldom-claimed promise, but a vital ingredient for those who want to follow Jesus. What are some of the sufferings that we can share with Him?
4. What can you do to help someone else have the same glorious experience?

5. Paul sought an *eternal experience* with Christ. He committed himself totally to this one great purpose: to attain to the resurrection of the dead (v.11). He was totally committed to that glorious day of redemption. He lived for that day and for that day alone.

What is so significant about the resurrection of the dead? What is to be so different about that day? At death, we go to be with the Lord. Quicker than the eye can blink, when our time comes, we shall stand face to face with Christ. What is the difference between meeting Christ then and the resurrection? Why did Paul long for the resurrection over and above his meeting the Lord at death? There are at least two significant reasons why the resurrection, the glorious day of redemption, takes precedence over our meeting the Lord at death.

a. The glorious day of resurrection will launch the events that will soon bring about the new heavens and earth. At death, when we go to be with the Lord, the world continues on in its sin and shame, disease and death, evil and corruption. *God is still being...*
   - cursed and dishonored.
   - denied and ignored.
   - rebelled against and rejected.

   But as stated, the resurrection will launch the events that bring about the glorious day of redemption—the new heavens and earth—the day when all evil and sin and the cursing and dishonor of God will be stopped. God will become All in All: worshipped and served in glory and majesty, dominion and power forever and ever.

b. The glorious day of resurrection will be the day when believers will have their earthly bodies transformed and recreated into perfect eternal bodies. At death when we go to be with the Lord, we do not receive our perfect eternal body. We will either be given temporary spiritual bodies or live with Christ as disembodied spirits. But as stated, at the resurrection the elements of our present bodies will be called forth by God from all over the world, and the elements shall be transformed into perfect and eternal bodies. And we shall live with God forever.

> "So also is the resurrection of the dead. It is sown in corruption; it is raised in incorruption: it is sown in dishonour; it is raised in glory: it is sown in weakness; it is raised in power: it is sown a natural body: it is raised a spiritual body. There is a natural body, and there is a spiritual body" (1 Cor.15:42-44).

ILLUSTRATION:
How hungry are you for the things of the Lord?

> *"In the Antarctic summer of 1908-09, Sir Ernest Shackleton and three companions attempted to travel to the South Pole from their winter quarters. They set off with four ponies, to help carry the load. Weeks later, their ponies dead, rations all but exhausted, they turned back toward their base, goal not accomplished. Altogether, they trekked 127 days.*
>
> *On the return journey, as Shackleton records in The Heart of the Antarctic, the time was spent talking about food---elaborate feasts, gourmet delights, sumptuous menus. As they staggered along, suffering from dysentery, not knowing whether they would survive, every waking hour was occupied with thoughts of eating.*

Jesus, who also knew the ravages of food deprivation, said, 'Blessed are those who hunger and thirst for righteousness.' We can understand Shackleton's obsession with food, which offers a glimpse of the passion Jesus intends for our quest for righteousness.[A]

QUESTION:
1. How would you rate your 'hunger' for the righteousness and knowledge of God?
   a. Starving—can't get enough.
   b. Hungry—but it will pass.
   c. Can take it or leave it.
   d. Stuffed—couldn't take another thing in.
   e. The sight of it makes me sick!

3. PAUL DID NOT COUNT HIMSELF AS HAVING YET ARRIVED—HE WAS NOT YET PERFECT (v.12-16).

Perfection is the great end for the believer. God has laid hold of the believer to make him perfect so that he can live and worship and serve Christ forever.

Now note a critical point: no person achieves perfection on this earth. The fact is so evident to the thinking and honest man that it is actually ridiculous to even make the statement. Yet, too many are so narrow in their thinking that they seldom if ever grasp what perfection would really mean. For example...

* Consider the brain and the mind. It has been estimated that man uses only *one-tenth of one percent* of his mental capacity. Imagine how far short this is of perfection!
* Consider the body. What would a perfect body be like? A body that never desired, thought, or did wrong; that never came up short; that never aged, deteriorated, died or decayed?

The examples could go on and on, but note what Paul says: he had not attained perfection. In fact, he was always emphasizing how far short he came.

> **"For I know that in me (that is, in my flesh,) dwelleth no good thing: for to will is present with me; but how to perform that which is good I find not. For the good that I would I do not: but the evil which I would not, that I do" (Ro.7:18-19).**

Beyond doubt, Paul was one of the greatest men who has ever lived. The great *Book of Second Corinthians* clearly shows this. If Paul was so short of perfection, how much further are we? The point bears repeating: no person achieves perfection on this earth. But note: Paul says five significant things.

1. Paul followed after perfection, after his God-given purpose (v.12). When Christ saved Paul, that was just the beginning, not the end. He had been saved to *live for Christ and to serve Christ*, and as long as he was on this earth he was going to *live for Christ* and do all he could *to serve Christ*. The word "follow after" means to press; to pursue just like a runner in a race. There was no place for walking, much less for sitting or lying around in comfort, complacency and lethargy.

⇒ Paul was going to do all he could to help the Lord in the great task of perfecting him.

APPLICATION:
There is no such thing as a genuine believer sitting still after he has been saved. The believer must not...
* become comfortable, complacent, lethargic, or lazy.
* waste time and lose opportunity.
* begin to think he is safe and secure forever; therefore, he can sometimes do what he likes and give in to his own desires.

The believer must follow, run, and press after perfection—the perfection for which Christ has saved him. The believer must be active in living for Christ.

"Know ye not that they which run in a race run all, but one receiveth the prize? So run, that ye may obtain. And every man that striveth for the mastery is temperate in all things. Now they do it to obtain a corruptible crown; but we an incorruptible. I therefore so run, not as uncertainly; so fight I, not as one that beateth the air: but I keep under my body, and bring it into subjection: lest that by any means, when I have preached to others, I myself should be a castaway" (1 Cor.9:24-27).

QUESTIONS:
1. What can you do to follow Christ more fully?
2. What kinds of things do you need to give up (or quit doing) in order to follow Christ more fully?

2. Paul worked at forgetting the past (v.13). This is a verse that is of enormous help to believers who have failed God—miserably failed Him. Paul had so failed God, and he was always confessing how far short he came (cp. Ro.7:18-19; 2 Cor.3:5; Eph.3:8). Paul faced what so many of us face:

⇒ failure and shortcoming
⇒ the struggle to forget it and to move on

How does a person do this? It is one of the most difficult things in all the world to do. And it is especially difficult if others are not forgiving and willing to let the believer put his failure behind him. But note: Paul tells us how to deal with the past. How? By concentrating and controlling the mind and by reaching forth to those things which are before us. Note the concentration and focus:

⇒ but *one thing*.
⇒ but *this one thing I do*.

In one focused act, we must forget the things that are past and reach forth to those things that are before us. The act involves two parts: both forgetting and reaching forth. The past cannot be forgotten without reaching forth to what lies ahead. A person cannot sit around moaning and regretting the past. To do so is to be concentrating upon the past. The things of the past are to be *forgotten*. The things of the future are to be the focus of the mind. The believer is to zero in on the things at hand and on the things that lie ahead. If we do this, there is no time to wallow around in the past and its failure.

"Strive to enter in at the strait gate: for many, I say unto you, will seek to enter in, and shall not be able" (Lk.13:24).

ILLUSTRATION:
"The believer should be future-oriented, 'forgetting those things which are behind.' Please keep in mind that in Bible terminology, 'to forget' does not mean 'to fail to remember.' Apart from senility, hypnosis, or a brain malfunction, no mature person can forget what has happened in the past. We may wish that we could erase certain bad memories, but we cannot. 'To forget' in the Bible means 'no longer to be influenced by or affected by.' When God promises, 'And their sins and iniquities will I remember no more' [Heb.10:17], He is not suggesting that He will conveniently have a bad memory! This is impossible with God. What God is saying is, 'I will no longer hold their sins against them. Their sins can no longer affect their standing with Me or influence My attitude toward them."[5]

QUESTIONS:
1. What are some of the sins that we as Christian believers work at forgetting?
2. Believers should forget every sin they have ever committed. How can you and your church help the repentant believer forget and put his sin behind him?

3. Does God forget our sins when we repent and seek His forgiveness? Explain your answer. (See Jer.31:34; Heb.8:12; 10:17; Micah 7:19.)

3. Paul pressed on toward the goal, toward God's purpose in Christ Jesus (v.14). What is God's purpose for us in Christ Jesus? It is to be conformed to the image of Christ—to be perfect even as He is perfect. Once we are perfect...
- we shall be incorruptible and eternal.
- we shall live in honor and glory.
- we shall live in God's perfect presence and power.
- we shall live in perfect righteousness and purity.
- we shall live worshipping and serving God eternally.

Perfection means eternal life, a perfect life that never ends—that goes on and on doing the things that God created us to do. Perfection means the eternal life of Jesus Christ—being conformed to the perfection of Jesus Christ.

"The Spirit itself beareth witness with our spirit, that we are the children of God: and if children, then heirs; heirs of God, and joint-heirs with Christ; if so be that we suffer with him, that we may be also glorified together" (Ro.8:16-17).

4. Paul kept his mind on growing and maturing in Christ (v.15). All believers are destined by God to be perfected in Christ Jesus, and we shall be perfected in the glorious day of redemption. We must keep our minds on perfection. Note: this is sometimes difficult to do because we live in a world that is gripped by the lust for...
- comfort and ease
- pleasure and plenty
- possessions and recognition
- indulgence and extravagance
- more and more

But note this fact: God will not let the genuine believer rest unless his mind is on righteousness and purity, the gospel and witnessing. God pricks our hearts, reveals that we are failing and coming short. God stirs us to get our minds back upon living like we should—upon pressing for perfection.

"Be ye therefore perfect, even as your Father which is in heaven is perfect" (Mt.5:48).

QUESTIONS:
1. Are you pressing for perfection, growing and maturing in Christ?
2. What kinds of things do you need to do in order to grow in Christ?

5. Paul maintained the growth he had already achieved (v.16). Too many live up and down lives. We gain some discipline and some growth, then before too long, we slip right back. It may involve...
- lying, stealing, or cheating
- devotions or prayer
- control of thoughts and mind
- discipline of body and habits

Growth takes place, but then some circumstance or interruption takes place, and the *new man* and new growth are forsaken and we slip back into being the *old man*, living just like we used to live.

But note the strong exhortation of Scripture: take what you have learned and attained and walk by that rule; keep your mind upon that rule.

"For to be carnally minded is death; but to be spiritually minded is life and peace" (Ro.8:6).

APPLICATION:

Paul _followed_ (after perfection).
Paul _worked_ (at forgetting the past).
Paul _pressed_ (on toward the goal).
Paul _kept_ (his mind on growing and maturing).
Paul _maintained_ (the growth he had achieved).

Do you get the picture? It takes effort, concentration, focus, and diligence to follow after Christ and His purpose for us. If any of these are neglected or let go, we will quickly slip back into sin and slip away from the goal of reaching perfection in Christ.

ILLUSTRATION:

J. Vernon McGee paints an excellent description of this passage for us:

> _"Now Paul, after receiving eternal life, is out running for a prize. Christ became everything to him, and he is running a race that he might win Christ. In what way? Well, someday he is going to appear in His presence. His whole thought is: 'When I come into His presence, I don't want to be ashamed.' John said that it is possible to be ashamed at His appearing._
>
> _"And now, little children, abide in him; that, when he shall appear, we may have confidence, and not be ashamed before him at his coming' [1 John 2:28]._
>
> _"There are a great many Christians today talking about wishing Christ would come, [but] if they really knew what it will mean to them, [they] would probably like to postpone it for awhile. If you think that you can live a careless Christian life and not have to answer for it, you are entirely wrong. One of these days you will have to stand before the judgment seat of Christ to give an account of the way you lived your life. I suggest that you get down on the racecourse and start living for Him."[6]_

QUESTIONS:

1. The Christian life is not easy. As you press on, what are some of the things that will oppose you and keep you from growing in Christ?
2. Our Christian growth should be steady. What things can you do to prevent extreme ups and downs?
3. When is your Christian growth the most consistent:
   a. During times of crisis?
   b. When your life has no major problems?

SUMMARY:

We have learned how Paul attempted to know God and have seen ways to apply these lessons to our own lives.

1. We must reject self-righteousness.
2. We must seek to win Christ—His righteousness, His perfection.
3. We must not count ourselves as having yet arrived—we are not yet perfect.

PHILIPPIANS 3:4-16

<u>PERSONAL JOURNAL NOTES:</u>
(Reflection & Response)

1. The most important thing that I learned from this lesson was:

2. The area that I need to work on the most is:

3. I can apply this lesson to my life by:

4. Closing Statement of Commitment:

---

[1] J. Vernon McGee, *Thru The Bible*, Vol.5, p.314.

[2] Kenneth Wuest, *Wuest's Word Studies In The Greek New Testament*, Vol.2 (Grand Rapids, MI: Eerdman's Publishing Co., 1966), p.91.

[3] J. Vernon McGee, *Thru The Bible*, Vol.5, p.314.

[4] Craig B. Larson, Editor,. *Illustrations for Preaching and Teaching*, p.199.

[5] Warren W. Wiersbe, *The Bible Exposition Commentary*, Vol.2, (Wheaton, IL: Victor Books, 1989), p.89.

[6] J. Vernon McGee. *Thru The Bible*, Vol.5, p.316.

107

	C. Pressing On: Marking Those Who Walk as Examples, 3:17-21	struction, whose God is their belly, and whose glory is in their shame, who mind earthly things.)	struction
			b. Their god: Appetite
			c. Their glory: Shameful
			d. Their mind: Earthly
		20 For our conversation is in heaven; from	3. Reason 3: The believer is a citizen of heaven
1. Reason 1: Some walk as good examples	17 Brethren, be followers together of	whence also we look	
a. Paul walked as an example	me, and mark them which walk so as ye	for the Saviour, the Lord Jesus Christ:	a. His life: Heaven centered
b. Others walked as examples	have us for an example.	21 Who shall change our vile body, that	b. His focus: The return of Christ
2. Reason 2: Many walk as enemies of the cross	18 (For many walk, of whom I have told you often, and now tell you even weeping, that they are enemies of the cross of Christ:	it may be fashioned like unto his glorious body, according to the working whereby he is able even to subdue all things unto himself.	c. His end: A changed body
a. Their end: De-	19 Whose end is de-		

Section IV
THE 'PRESSING ON' OF THE CHRISTIAN BELIEVER,
Philippians 3:1-21

Study 3: **PRESSING ON: MARKING THOSE WHO WALK AS EXAMPLES**

Text: Philippians 3:17-21

Aim: To follow the positive examples set before us, not the negative.

Memory Verse:
"For our conversation [citizenship] is in heaven; whence also we look for the Saviour, the Lord Jesus Christ" (Philippians 3:20).

INTRODUCTION:
How many times have we heard parents tell their children, "Don't do as I do; just do as I say"? Unfortunately, we hear the same conversation take place in the church. It has been said that the clearest sermon spoken is spoken by our actions. Where are the teachers of the faith: those men and women who instruct by a godly example?

Your life is a sermon. What kind of example are you setting for those who follow you?

This is one of the most important passages in the Bible. It has to do with the example we set before the world and before our families and friends. The way we live and what we do influences people. We may not want to influence them, but it does not matter whether we want to or not: they are influenced. Family, friends, and children—everyone who knows us—watch us; and they follow both the good and the bad of our example. It may be conscious or unconscious, intentional or unintentional, but we influence people by how we live and by what we do.
⇒ If we follow good and do good, it encourages them to do good.
⇒ If we follow bad and do bad, it sets a pattern of bad before others. It even causes some (in particular, the young and immature) to think that since we did it and still got along fairly well, they can do it and get along fairly well, too.

The point is this: the life we live sets a pattern for others to follow. Others are going to follow us no matter what we do. This says something to us, something of critical importance: we must live lives on the highest plane possible. We must set the most dynamic example possible.

We must set the most perfect pattern possible for others to follow. But it also says something else: we must follow after those who live on the highest plane of life. We must mark those who walk as examples and follow after the great traits of their lives. We must take those who live as good examples and dissect the traits of their lives, applying those traits to our own lives. This is the subject of the present passage: marking those who walk as examples for us all.

OUTLINE:
1. Reason 1: some walk as good examples (v.17).
2. Reason 2: many walk as enemies of the cross (v.18-19).
3. Reason 3: the believer is a citizen of heaven (v.20-21).

1. REASON 1: SOME WALK AS GOOD EXAMPLES (v.17).

We must first mark those who walk as good examples. Note what Paul said: he and others followed Christ ever so diligently; therefore, they were dynamic examples as to how people should walk and live. When a person lives a life on the highest plane—when he lives like Christ said to live—he is a good example. He is living just like we all should live.

What did Paul mean? Was he claiming perfection—claiming to be the perfect pattern for men to follow? No! A thousand times no! In fact, the very opposite is true. He had just declared...
* that he could never stand before God in his own righteousness (v.9).
* that he had not yet attained (v.12).
* that he was not perfect (v.12).
* that he had not apprehended that for which Christ had laid hold of him (v.13).

What then did Paul mean? Just what he said. He was a dynamic example...
* in forgetting the things that were past (v.13).
* in reaching forth to the things that lay ahead (v.13).
* in pressing toward the prize, even the high calling of God in Christ Jesus (v.14).

Paul was a dynamic example in seeking to follow Christ. He was forever reaching forth, forever pressing to be like Christ. He never reached the perfect pattern of Christ—he could not, not as long as he was a man—but he pressed and pressed to be all he could for Christ. It is this that Paul sets before us as a pattern. We are to follow Paul...
* in forgetting the past, no matter how terrible it is (v.13).
* in reaching forth to the things that lie ahead (v.13).
* in pressing toward the prize, even the high calling of God in Christ Jesus (v.14).

We will never achieve perfection, not in this life, but we are to follow after Christ and seek to be like Him. Now note the point: when we see a person sharing Christ with such dynamic commitment and energy, that person is an example for us. We should follow that person. He is following after Christ, doing the very thing we should be doing.

Note the word "example." The underlying meaning of the word is that of an imprint or mark made by a blow or some mould or dye. The idea is that we are to be seeking Christ with such diligence that our example will be like a powerful blow being thrown at those around us. Take the most powerful boxing blow of the heavyweight champion, and our example for Christ should strike others with just as much power.

APPLICATION:
No believer should ever claim or think that he has come anywhere close to perfection. But *every believer* should follow Christ with so much commitment and diligence that he is a dynamic example for others. Every believer should be able to say "follow me"—follow my seeking after Christ—my seeking to be like Christ.

"Be ye followers of me, even as I also am of Christ" (1 Cor.11:1).

ILLUSTRATION:

Are people drawn to you because of your witness? Is your life like that flame which draws the moth near?

Martin was that kind of a believer. He was a medical doctor by occupation, but he was a spiritual doctor in the more important field of life. He was cut out of the same mold as two other physicians who made a significant impact on this sin-sick world--Luke the physician from the New Testament, and the Lord Jesus Himself, the Great Physician.

A gray and gentle saint, Martin's loving eyes and captivating smile would overcome the most resistant soul. Assuredly, God shared Martin with this world in order to help heal the lonely wounds in each life he crossed.

It was no surprise that children of all ages wanted to be around him. Seldom would there be an empty seat by Martin. Why? Why did people want to be near Martin? To put it very simply, he loved people. And people need to be loved above all else.

Are you approachable to others? Are there any empty seats near you?

QUESTIONS:
1. Are people drawn to you because of your witness?
2. Are people attracted by Christ-like features in your life: strength, love, joy, peace, gentleness, giving, and caring?
3. No matter what your position or social standing in life is, your daily walk with Christ is what will speak volumes to people. Your life is what will make people want to be around you and follow your example. Are you setting a good, Christ-like example for others or are you leading others away from Christ with your lifestyle?

2. REASON 2: MANY WALK AS ENEMIES OF THE CROSS (v.18-19).

Who are the enemies of the cross? Many commentators say they are the hypocritical and false believers within the church, those who are nominal Christians. They say that the word "walk" is used of Christians in verse 17; therefore, it also refers to church members in verse 18. It is also said that Paul would weep only for false believers within the church.

It is true that Paul could have been referring to false and hypocritical believers within the church; however, every unbeliever both in and out of the church walks as an enemy of the cross...

- whether the leader of a nation or a movement who is set on wiping out the church and the cross.
- whether a professing believer who really doubts the substitutionary death and resurrection of Jesus Christ.

Note something else as well: it is a common thing for believers to weep for the lost. Certainly Paul wept many times over the lost of the world and not just over false believers within the church.

> "I exhort therefore, that, first of all, supplications, prayers, intercessions, and giving of thanks, be made for all men; for kings, and for all that are in authority; that we may lead a quiet and peaceable life in all godliness and honesty. For this is good and acceptable in the sight of God our Saviour; who will have all men to be saved, and to come unto the knowledge of the truth" (1 Tim.2:1-4).

Again, who are the enemies of the cross? It seems best to take the verse for just what it says: there are many who walk as "the enemies of the cross"—no matter who they are, whether within or without the church. Unquestionably, the enemies of the cross are many. Note what is said about them.

1. *Their end is destruction*. The word means perdition, destroyed, or slayed; to lose one's well-being; to be wasted, ruined, and given a worthless existence. It does not mean that a person will cease to exist. It means a person will be destroyed and devastated and condemned to a worthless existence. He will suffer waste, loss, and ruin forever and ever.

If a person stands as an enemy of the cross, he shall be destroyed. It does not matter who he is, either within or without the church, he shall suffer perdition, that is, utter destruction. Who is an enemy of the cross? It is the person...

- who rejects the cross of Christ as the only way to God.
- who does not accept the death of Christ as payment for his sins.
- who does not believe that Christ died for him, that is, as the punishment for his transgressions.
- who does not believe that the penalty for his imperfection was borne by Christ on the cross.
- who does not approach God claiming that he is coming by the death of Christ—that is, that he wants God to accept him in the death of Christ.
- who considers the cross of Christ to be foolishness.
- who opposes and curses Christ and His cross.
- who persecutes and attempts to stamp out Christ and His cross.

"For the preaching of the cross is to them that perish foolishness; but unto us which are saved it is the power of God" (1 Cor.1:18).

2. *Their god is their belly*, that is, their appetite, their sensuality, their desire for the physical pleasures of this world. Physical and material gratification is their god. They center their lives around...

- possessions and property
- houses and furnishings
- food and appetite
- comfort and plenty
- money and wealth
- pleasure and sex
- acceptance and social standing
- position and success
- honor and fame

Just take a moment to think about any of the above, how some persons center and focus their lives upon such things. Some persons spend more time in front of a mirror or eating or thinking about acceptance, success, possessions, or some business deal than they do in prayer.

The point is this: when a person has a craving and an appetite for such things, they become his god. The craving begins to consume his thoughts, energy, and effort. Before long his craving is taking up so much of his energy that he has very little if any time for God or for anything else. His appetite and craving, or as the Scripture says, his belly, becomes his god.

"For they that are after the flesh do mind the things of the flesh; but they that are after the Spirit the things of the Spirit. For to be carnally minded is death; but to be spiritually minded is life and peace" (Ro.8:5-6).

3. *Their glory is their shame*. This simply means that men boast in their sins and shame. They boast in and pride themselves in...

- their comfort
- their drunkenness
- their gluttony
- their conquests
- their sex
- their partying
- what they eat
- what they have purchased
- their authority and power
- their possessions

"And he said unto them, Take heed, and beware of covetousness: for a man's life consisteth not in the abundance of the things which he possesseth" (Lk.12:15).

4. *They keep their mind on earthly things*. This is simply another way of saying that a person is worldly. He focuses his mind, energy and effort upon the things of the world. But note:

the things of the world include much more than the physical and material gratifications of this world. Worldly things also include the commendable things that are accepted by society such as...

- religions and spiritual pursuits
- self-development programs
- rules of virtue and morality
- the pursuit of ambition or success
- employment and jobs and business

As stated, such things are commendable and some are even necessary for survival and health. But the point is this: the basis of our lives must be the cross of Christ not the things of this world. The only hope for conquering the ills and corruption of society and the evil and death of man is the cross of Christ. Nothing on this earth, no matter how good and beneficial it is, can give us life—not abundant and eternal life. Only Jesus Christ can give us life that conquers all and that infuses us with life that lasts forever. Therefore, the focus of our lives must be Christ and His cross. The person who sets his mind on earthly things is an enemy of the cross of Christ.

> "And be not conformed to this world: but be ye transformed by the renewing of your mind, that ye may prove what is that good, and acceptable, and perfect, will of God" (Ro.12:2).

QUESTIONS:
1. What makes a person become an enemy of the cross?
2. How can you protect yourself, your family, and your church from the enemies of the cross?
3. How can you effectively witness to an enemy of the cross?

3. REASON 3: THE BELIEVER IS A CITIZEN OF HEAVEN (v.20-21).

Note three points.
1. The believer's life is to be heaven-centered, for his citizenship is in heaven. The word "conversation" means *citizenship* in this context. Remember that Philippi was a Roman colony and its citizens, although in Macedonia, were citizens of Rome. As pointed out earlier, the citizens of Roman colonies lived as Romans: they dressed as Romans, spoke the Roman language, lived by the laws of Rome, engaged in Roman pleasures and social affairs, and worshipped the Roman gods. Despite the fact that they lived in Macedonia, their citizenship was in Rome.

The point to see is this: the Philippian believers knew exactly what it meant to live in one place and to be a citizen of another place. They knew exactly what it would mean to live upon the earth and...

- to dress as a citizen of heaven and not of the earth.
- to speak as a citizen of heaven and not of the earth.
- to engage in the pleasures of a citizen of heaven and not of the earth.
- to live by the laws of heaven as well as the laws of earth.
- to worship the God of heaven and not the religions and gods of this earth.

APPLICATION:
Believers of all generations are to live as citizens of heaven and not of this world. The point is forceful. We are to separate from the world and its evil influence, setting our sights on heaven. We should consider this world as a temporary home only, not a permanent dwelling place. That should help us to focus upon our heavenly citizenship and to turn away from the things of this earth that will eventually pass away.

> "Now therefore ye are no more strangers and foreigners, but fellow-citizens with the saints, and of the household of God" (Eph.2:19).

2.   The believer's life is to be focused upon the return of Christ. He is to be looking for the Lord's return—constantly looking—looking every day of his life.

ILLUSTRATION:
Lehman Strauss makes a strong point in the following:

> *"The greatest event in any country on earth is a visit from its chief emperor. History records the most elaborate preparations and memorials for such an event. Special coins have been minted, commemorative stamps issued, and highways built. Looking forward to the Coming of our Lord Jesus Christ is the highlight of Christian expectation. We should be dwelling daily in this thought of His return....Imagine how the residents in your neighborhood would feel if the President of the United States had announced that he was making a personal appearance in your community. I feel certain there would be some special preparations for his coming."*[1]

APPLICATION:
Should our anticipation and preparation be any less than the above mentioned illustration for the Savior of the world? No! There should be no comparison—the return of Jesus Christ deserves our utmost and constant attention.

> **"Therefore be ye also ready: for in such an hour as ye think not the Son of man cometh" (Mt.24:44).**

3.   The believer's life is to focus upon the glorious body he is to receive when Christ returns.

a.   Right now the believer's body is vile, that is, lowly and humiliating...
   - because it has its origin out of the earth: it is nothing more than earthly chemicals or human flesh.
   - because it is subject to sin and selfishness, evil and destruction.
   - because it is so weak: it becomes sick and diseased, injured and maimed, aged and deteriorated.
   - because it is corruptible and dying, aging and mortal, offering no hope of eternal life

b.   However, note the wonderful declaration: the Lord Jesus Christ shall change the believer's body, making it just like His glorious body. Imagine! To have a body that is permanent, constant, and unchanging. The believer will receive a spiritual body.

> **"Who shall change our vile body, that it may be fashioned like unto his glorious body, according to the working whereby he is able even to subdue all things unto himself" (Ph.3:21).**

c.   How is such possible? By the power of God, the very power which is able to subdue all things to Christ. The very power that created the world and all that is in the world...
   - is sovereign over the world.
   - is able to control the world.
   - is able to subdue the world.
   - is able to recreate the world.
   - is able to transform the body of man.

QUESTIONS:
1.   What difference does it make if we are citizens of heaven or of earth?
2.   What are some things we can do to help us focus upon the Lord's return?
3.   Jesus Christ could return any moment. How should this fact affect the way we live?

SUMMARY:

As we have studied the example of Paul and others, we must learn to:
1. Walk as good examples.
2. Avoid the enemies of the cross.
3. Focus on our heavenly citizenship.

PERSONAL JOURNAL NOTES:
(Reflection & Response)

1. The most important thing that I learned from this lesson was:

2. The area that I need to work on the most is:

3. I can apply this lesson to my life by:

4. Closing Statement Of Commitment:

---

[1] Lehman Strauss, *Devotional Studies in Philippians*, p.207f.

	CHAPTER 4	and beseech Syntyche, that they be of the same mind in the Lord.	through agreement & unity
	V. THE SECRET OF PEACE--THE PEACE OF GOD HIMSELF, 4:1-9		a. The plea: For arguers to agree in the Lord
		3 And I entreat thee also, true yokefellow, help those women which laboured with me in the gospel, with Clement also, and with other my fellowlabourers, whose names are in the book of life.	b. The need: The help of a true friend
	A. The Steps to Peace (Part I): Standing Fast, Unity, Rejoicing, & Gentleness, 4:1-5		1) Must help them because they were co-laborers
			2) Must help them because their names are in the Book of Life
1. Step 1: Peace comes through standing fast	Therefore, my brethren dearly beloved and longed for, my joy and crown, so stand fast in the Lord, my dearly beloved.	4 Rejoice in the Lord always: and again I say, Rejoice.	3. Step 3: Peace comes through rejoicing continually & repeatedly
a. The source of strength: Being "in the Lord"			
b. The encouragement: A brother who cares		5 Let your moderation be known unto all men. The Lord is at hand.	4. Step 4: Peace comes through a strong gentleness
2. Step 2: Peace comes	2 I beseech Euodias,		

Section V
THE SECRET OF PEACE—THE PEACE OF GOD HIMSELF,
Philippians 4:1-9

Study 1: **THE STEPS TO PEACE (PART I): STANDING FAST, UNITY, REJOICING, & GENTLENESS**

Text: **Philippians 4:1-5**

Aim: To learn the steps to securing peace in your life.

Memory Verse:
> "Rejoice in the Lord always: and again I say rejoice" (Philippians 4:4).

SECTION INTRODUCTION:

The point of this whole passage (4:1-9) is the peace of God (v.7) and the presence of the God of peace (v.9[b]). There are six steps that a believer must take to maintain the peace of God within his heart and life. If the believer fails to take these steps, he grieves both the Lord and fellow believers, those who have made a special contribution to his growth, those who look upon him as their "joy and crown" (Ph.4:1). Unfortunately, when a believer loses his peace with God, several things happen...

- He becomes self-conscious, sheepishly shy and guilty, and perhaps discouraged and defeated.
- He becomes cantankerous, critical, and divisive.
- He begins to slip back into sin.

The peace he once had with God and man becomes disturbed, and restlessness grips his soul. His restlessness stirs him into being a troublemaker or into sin or else it plummets him into despair and defeat. He has failed; therefore, he feels unworthy and unable to walk victoriously with God. This is the importance of this passage: the secret of peace—the peace of God Himself.

PHILIPPIANS 4:1-5

INTRODUCTION:

What kind of value do you place on having peace? Billy Graham writes about the value of peace:

> *"I know men who would write a check for a million dollars if they could find peace. Millions are searching for it. Every time they get close to finding the peace that you have found in Christ, Satan steers them away. He blinds them. He throws up a smoke screen. He bluffs them. And they miss it! But you have found it! It is yours now forever. You have found the secret of life."*[1]

This passage (4:1-5) is speaking to Christian believers, not to unbelievers. Unbelievers do not have peace with God. They reject, question, deny, curse, and oppose God. God feels no peace between Himself and an unbeliever. No matter how mild the unbeliever's questioning and rejection is, it is still questioning and rejection and not peace. But when an unbeliever surrenders his life and accepts God, peace is made between him and God. Peace rules both within and between the person and God. In fact, God causes a flood of peace to surge through the heart and life of the new believer.

The question is this: once we have the peace of God flooding our lives, how do we maintain that peace? How do we keep the peace of God ruling and reigning within our souls? How do we stay aware that God's very own presence is within us—stay aware that the God of peace lives within our very being? This is the discussion of this passage: the steps to peace.

OUTLINE:
1. Step 1: peace comes through standing fast (v.1).
2. Step 2: peace comes through agreement and unity (v.2-3).
3. Step 3: peace comes through rejoicing continually and repeatedly (v.4).
4. Step 4: peace comes through a strong gentleness (v.5).

1. STEP 1: PEACE COMES THRU STANDING FAST (v.1).

This verse is a transitional verse between what has been said and what is about to be said. Paul has just said...
- there are enemies of the cross of Christ,
- the believer's citizenship is in heaven,
- the Lord is going to return and take us out of this world into heaven, transforming our bodies;

...therefore, *stand fast in the Lord.*

However, note how the verse fits in with what is to follow. Verse nine is the conclusion of this section:

> **"Those things, which ye have both learned, and received, and heard, and seen in me, do: and the God of peace shall be with you" (v.9).**

If a person wants the *God of peace*, he must do the things which Paul taught and did, and one of the major things he taught was to stand fast in the Lord. The word "stand fast" means simply to stand firm, to persist, to persevere. It is the picture of a soldier standing fast against the onslaught of an enemy. He refuses to give ground no matter the pressure and strength of attack. He does not flinch; he is not unstable, and he is never defeated. The Christian believer is to stand fast...
- no matter how great the trial
- no matter the pressure of the temptation
- no matter the influence, offer, and allurement made by others

But how does a believer stand fast? When the temptation to surrender is so appealing and the trial is so terrible, where can the believer find the strength to stand fast? There are two places.

116

1.   There is the believer's source of strength: the Lord Himself. Note the words, "Stand fast _in the Lord_." There is only one place the believer can stand fast, and that is "_in the Lord_." The believer must be living and moving and having his being in the Lord; that is, he must be...

- praying, talking, and sharing with the Lord all day long.
- keeping his thoughts upon the Lord: the glorious salvation, hope, and mission He has given believers.
- serving and ministering for the Lord, bearing testimony of Him and meeting the needs of those who hurt and need help.

When a believer is walking _in the Lord_ throughout the day, his mind and thoughts are upon the Lord. Therefore, when the temptations and trials come, he is _conscious and aware of the Lord's presence and strength._ He has been thinking and sharing and talking with the Lord—standing and walking in the Lord—all day long; therefore, he is much more able to stand fast against the temptation and trial. This is exactly what is meant by being "in the Lord."

⇒   Believers are to be walking in prayer and praise all day long. This is what keeps the peace of God dwelling in their lives—the "peace of God" that conquers all trials and temptations.

> **"Be careful for nothing; but in every thing by prayer and supplication with thanksgiving let your requests be made known unto God. And the peace of God, which passeth all understanding, shall keep your hearts and minds through Christ Jesus" (Ph.4:6).**

⇒   Believers are to be walking with their minds upon the Lord and the things that are pure and honorable. This is what gives them a sense that the "God of peace" walks with them—the God of peace who gives the believer the power to conquer all trials and temptations.

> **"Finally, brethren, whatsoever things are true, whatsoever things are honest, whatsoever things are just, whatsoever things are pure, whatsoever things are lovely, whatsoever things are of good report; if there be any virtue, and if there be any praise, think on these things. Those things, which ye have both learned, and received, and heard, and seen in me, do: and the God of peace shall be with you" (Ph.4:8-9).**

⇒   Believers are to actually work at bringing every single thought into subjection to Christ.

> **"Casting down imaginations, and every high thing that exalteth itself against the knowledge of God, and bringing into captivity every thought to the obedience of Christ" (2 Cor.10:5).**

APPLICATION:

The believer who prays and keeps his mind and thoughts upon the Lord is the believer who stands fast in the Lord. Common sense tells us this. There is no way a person can "do his own thing" day in and day out and expect to remain "in the Lord." There must be open lines of communication to experience the peace and presence of God.

QUESTIONS:

1. How much of your day do you spend in prayer, meditation, and thinking on the things of God? Is it in proportion to what He's done for you?
2. What things distract you from experiencing the peace and presence of God?
3. How can you focus your mind on the things that are...

• true	• lovely
• honest	• of good report
• just	• virtuous
• pure	• praise-worthy

2. There is the encouragement: a minister or brother who loves and cares about his fellow-believer's standing fast. Note how Paul, the minister, feels about his flock—how deeply he feels for those under his care:

⇒ my dearly beloved brothers.
⇒ whom I long to see.
⇒ my joy and crown.

    a. He calls them my "dearly beloved brothers": they were his brothers and sisters in Christ. They had all trusted Christ as their Savior and become sons and daughters of the family of God. They were all brothers and sisters of the Lord, and Paul is reminding them of this relationship. Therefore, they should all stand fast in the Lord.

    b. He says that he longs to see them. He is in prison unable to be with them, but his heart is with his dear family, the family of God. Therefore, they need to please his heart by standing fast.

    c. He says they are his "joy and crown." This is probably a reference to the rewards to be given in the glorious day of redemption. The word "crown" refers to the crown or wreath that was given and sat upon the head of a victorious athlete after he had won the victor's crown in his particular event. Paul says that his joy and crown will be the lives of the Philippians themselves when they all appear before Christ. Therefore, if he was to receive the joy and crown of their presence, they must stand fast in the Lord.

    The thing to see is this: the need of believers for personal encouragement. If believers are to stand fast, they must be loved and cared for by the minister and other believers. Nothing encourages us any more than knowing that we are loved and cared for by others. The love of others stirs us to live like we should and to stand fast against temptation and trial.

APPLICATION:
Scripture exhorts believers to stand fast in several things.
1) Believers are to stand fast in the faith.

    "Watch ye, stand fast in the faith, quit you like men, be strong"(1 Cor.16:13).

2) Believers are to stand fast in the liberty of Christ.

    "Stand fast therefore in the liberty wherewith Christ hath made us free, and be not entangled again with the yoke of bondage" (Gal.5:1).

3) Believers are to stand fast in one spirit, striving together for the faith of the gospel.

    "Only let your conversation be as it becometh the gospel of Christ: that whether I come and see you, or else be absent, I may hear of your affairs, that ye stand fast in one spirit, with one mind striving together for the faith of the gospel" (Ph.1:27).

4) Believers are to stand fast in the Lord which is the secret of peace.

    "Therefore, my brethren dearly beloved and longed for, my joy and crown, so stand fast in the Lord, my dearly beloved" (Ph.4:1).

5) Believers are to stand fast in holding the teachings or doctrines that have been taught.

> **"Therefore, brethren, stand fast, and hold the traditions [things] which ye have been taught, whether by word, or our epistle" (2 Th.2:15).**

QUESTIONS:
1. What does it mean to "stand fast in the Lord"?
2. What are some barriers that keep believers from standing fast?
3. What can we do to combat the enticements of a fleshly, materialistic society and remain strong in the Lord?

2. STEP 2: PEACE COMES THRU AGREEMENT & UNITY (v.2-3).

There is no peace if people are...
- arguing
- bickering
- biting
- brawling
- wrangling
- disputing
- dissenting
- grumbling
- criticizing

Paul knew this, a fact that is easily seen by all but too often ignored by some. Paul knew something else as well, something that the Lord Himself knew. There were some in the Philippian church who were being critical, arguing, grumbling, and quarreling. The Lord had already had Paul to charge the believers:

⇒ To stand fast in one spirit and in defending the gospel.

> **"Only let your conversation be as it becometh the gospel of Christ: that whether I come and see you, or else be absent, I may hear of your affairs, that ye stand fast in one spirit, with one mind striving together for the faith of the gospel" (Ph.1:27).**

⇒ To love each other and to be of one accord and mind.

> **"If there be therefore any consolation in Christ, if any comfort of love, if any fellowship of the Spirit, if any bowels and mercies, fulfil ye my joy, that ye be likeminded, having the same love, being of one accord, of one mind" (Ph.2:1-2).**

⇒ To esteem others better than self.

> **"Let nothing be done through strife or vainglory; but in lowliness of mind let each esteem other better than themselves. Look not every man on his own things, but every man also on the things of others" (Ph.2:3-4).**

1. The plea is for all quarrelers to agree in the Lord (v.2). The source of the disturbance in the church was due to two prominent ladies in the church: Euodia and Syntyche. Who they were and what caused the trouble between them is not known. Only one thing is known about them: they were quarrelers—two women who differed and who bickered and argued, criticized and dissented, murmured and grumbled.

Note what Paul did: he pleaded for the two ladies to get their minds together "in the Lord." As stated in the former point, if a person is living and moving and having his being "in the Lord," then he is walking and serving the Lord. He is consumed with the Lord and His mission. There is no time for arguing and divisiveness. In fact, the very opposite is true. He has time only for joining hands with others who are living and moving in the Lord—all seeking to fulfil the Lord's mission upon earth. A person walking in the Lord is consumed with keeping the presence of the Lord alive in his heart and life. His thoughts are upon the Lord and His mission, not upon differences with other believers and arguing and divisiveness.

2.   The need is for a true friend, a yokefellow, to step in and help any who are quarreling (v.3). The word "yokefellow" is thought by some to be a proper name given to some Christians when they were baptized. It was a common practice for believers to be given new names at their baptism in order to symbolize their spiritual birth. Just who this yokefellow was is not known, but he must have been a man deeply respected by the people of the church. His name refers to the *yoke* or *collar* that was fitted around the neck of oxen for plowing. The collar attached the plow, holding the two oxen together so that they would pull together, getting the work done more quickly. Therefore, "yokefellow" means a person who pulls and works cooperatively with others. The very fact that Paul would ask him to help the two quarreling ladies shows that he was highly esteemed. Paul felt that he cared and that the two quarrelers would listen to him—that he could solve the dispute to bring about reconciliation.

APPLICATION:

Most churches have one or more *yokefellows*, persons...
- who love and care deeply for others.
- who are always helping and ministering to others.
- whom God has gifted and appointed to be helpers to the flock.
- who are highly respected and esteemed by most in the congregation.

The yokefellow is the person who should step in when quarrels and divisiveness begin to arouse their poisonous heads. The yokefellow is the person especially gifted by God to bring reconciliation and peace to the church.

Note: a message is given to the yokefellow as well as to the two quarrelers. The yokefellow is to help; helping is not an option. God had called and gifted him with a loving and caring nature that was especially suited for this kind of ministry. Therefore, he was to use his gift by stepping forward and doing his best to bring reconciliation and peace. Note also: there are two other reasons why he must help.

⇒   The quarrelers were co-laborers in the gospel. They had helped Paul and Clement and others in the church. They needed to be serving in the gospel, not arguing and differing. Therefore, every effort possible had to be exerted in trying to salvage them.

⇒   Second, their names were in the Book of Life. They were true believers who had slipped back into a life of sinful divisiveness. Despite their sin, they were true believers; therefore, every effort needed to be made to restore them.

"With good will doing service, as to the Lord, and not to men" (Eph.6:7).

"Brethren, if a man be overtaken in a fault, ye which are spiritual, restore such an one in the spirit of meekness; considering thyself, lest thou also be tempted. Bear ye one another's burdens, and so fulfil the law of Christ" (Gal.6:1-2).

QUESTIONS:
1. Have you ever been a divisive person in the church?
2. Have you ever been at odds with or hurt another believer?
3. When there is trouble between believers or division in the church, what needs to be done? (See Mt.18:15-20.)
4. Is there a need for a 'yokefellow' in your church, someone to patch things up or mend some hurt feelings? Can you identify any 'yokefellows' in your church?
5. What qualities does a true 'yokefellow' have?
6. Has God called you to be a "yokefellow"?

3. STEP 3: PEACE COMES THRU REJOICING CONTINUALLY AND REPEATEDLY (v.4).

Note that a person is to rejoice always, that is, continually; and then he is to rejoice again, that is, repeatedly.

Remember: Paul is in prison, and the church is having a problem with some false teaching. Yet, Paul challenges the believers: they are to walk about rejoicing in the Lord. In fact they are to rejoice in the Lord always—no matter the circumstances.

ILLUSTRATION:

Are you waiting for your circumstances to improve before you begin to rejoice? Is your ability to rejoice related to your happiness? Dr. J. Vernon McGee shares this humorous story about what it means to radiate joy. Is your joy radiating?

> *"The Fuller brush man calls at our house on Saturdays. He is not a sorrowful fellow by any means. I don't know whether he is having trouble at home or not, but he sure radiates joy. One Saturday morning my wife had gone to the market, and from my study window I saw him coming. I thought, I'll ignore him because I'm busy, and I'm not going to fool with brushes today. So he came and pushed the doorbell. I let him push it. He pushed it two or three times. I thought, He'll leave now. But he didn't leave. He knew somebody was in the house, so he just put his thumb down on the doorbell and held it.*
>
> *"Finally in self-defense I had to go to the door. When I opened the door, I expected him to be a little irritated because I had made him wait. But no, he was happy about it. Everything pleased him. He greeted my joyfully,*
>
> *"'Dr. McGee, I didn't expect to see you today!' With a scowl I said, 'My wife has gone to the market. She'll see you the next time you are around.' But that wasn't enough for him. I do not know how he did it, but in the next ten seconds he was in the living room and I was holding a little brush in my hand. Then I couldn't order him out—he'd given me a little brush. And so I stood there listening to his sales pitch.*
>
> *"When he had finished, I said, 'Now look, I don't buy brushes and I don't need one. My wife generally buys from you, and she'll probably buy next time, but I haven't time to look at them. I'm busy this morning.' So he thanked me and started down the walkway whistling! You would have thought I had bought every brush he had! I met a man who trains Fuller brush salesmen, and I told him about this experience. He said that they were so instructed; they are trained to radiate joy.*
>
> *"Now I do not know if that Fuller brush man was happy or not, but a child of God ought to have real joy, the joy of the Lord, in his life."[2]*

APPLICATION:

Continual rejoicing is impossible if our focus is not on Christ. Our decision to rejoice is not linked to the quality of our circumstances. Our decision to rejoice is based upon the Lord of our circumstances.

QUESTIONS:
1. What are some circumstances that occasionally get the best of you?
2. What practical things can you do to develop a habit of rejoicing?

4. STEP 4: PEACE COMES THRU A STRONG GENTLENESS (v.5).

The word "moderation" is a difficult word to translate into English. It is translated by others as gentleness, forbearance, reasonableness, consideration, agreeableness, courtesy, patience, and softness. There is a tendency to say that either forbearance or gentleness is the better translation.

1. Believers are to be gentle and forbearing in dealing with unbelievers. Note the phrase, "all men." The exhortation not only deals with believers within the church, but with unbelievers (v.5).

PHILIPPIANS 4:1-5

APPLICATION:
William Barclay makes an excellent point:

> "The Christian, as Paul sees it, is the man who knows that for him there is something beyond justice. When the woman taken in adultery was brought before Him, Jesus could have applied the letter of the Law, and she should, according to it, have been stoned; but He went beyond justice. As far as justice goes, there is not one of us who deserves anything but the condemnation of God, but God goes far beyond justice. Paul lays it down that the mark of a Christian in his personal relationships with his fellow-men must be that he knows when, and when not, to insist on justice, and that he always remembers that there is something which is beyond justice, and which makes a man like God."[3]

We must be gentle and forbearing in dealing with unbelievers. The last thing we must do is criticize, condemn, censor, neglect, and ignore unbelievers. We must reach out to the world with the gospel, treating them with a *loving gentleness*. We must be gentle, having absolutely nothing to do with harshness. Too many of us are harsh and critical or neglectful and withdrawn. Too many of us are wrapped in the cloak of religion having nothing to do with reaching out to the lost. The desperate need of the hour is for us to reach out with the gospel in a spirit of *love and gentleness*.

> "**Forbearing** one another, and forgiving one another, if any man have a quarrel against any: even as Christ forgave you, so also do ye" (Col.3:13).

2.   The reason we must be gentle to men is because the Lord is at hand (v.5). He is ready to come, and His coming is near. This simply means that when He comes, everyone of us will need Him to treat us with gentleness. We are sinners—men and women, boys and girls—who sin too often. The Lord will have every right to be critical and condemning of us. Our only hope is that He will be gentle with us. Therefore, we must be gentle with all other men. Only if we are forgiving toward them will the Lord be forgiving toward us.

> "For if ye forgive men their trespasses, your heavenly Father will also forgive you: but if ye forgive not men their trespasses, neither will your Father forgive your trespasses" (Mt.6:14-15).

ILLUSTRATION:
Have you wanted to steamroll someone lately? You feel they've had it coming for a long time and your patience has run out? Listen to this story:

The classroom became steamy as the heated debate grew more intense with each passing moment. The professor was a meek-looking sort of fellow; sort of short in stature but long on patience.

The arguing student had the audacity to try and prove the mild-mannered professor wrong. Brains were not a gift of this particular student for two reasons:
⇒ One, he had all the facts about the subject mixed-up—he was just flat-out wrong.
⇒ Two, he was challenging a man who was a leading authority in the field.

After hearing enough, the professor with a frown upon his face spoke sharply: "*I know enough about this subject to blow you out of the water.*"

The class sat in absolute silence, waiting for a pen to drop (his pen signing the expulsion papers of the arguing student).

In a soft voice, the professsor, humbly apologized to the class for his outburst. "*I had no right to say what I said.*"

What the professor said that day spoke volumes, picturing exactly what God expects from His followers. God wants followers who are gentle: followers who have mastered the art of "strength under control."

PHILIPPIANS 4:1-5

QUESTIONS:
1. People suffer the blast from men of strength everyday. They are intimidated either physically, intellectually, emotionally, or spiritually. What can you do in your life to become more gentle?
2. Who needs your gentle touch today? What are some things you can do to touch their lives this week?

SUMMARY:

There are certain steps that are key to achieving peace. We must remember that:
1. Peace comes through standing fast.
2. Peace comes through agreement and unity.
3. Peace comes through rejoicing continually & repeatedly.
4. Peace comes through a strong gentleness.

PERSONAL JOURNAL NOTES:
(Reflection & Response)

1. The most important thing that I learned from this lesson was:

2. The area that I need to work on the most is:

3. I can apply this lesson to my life by:

4. Closing Statement of Commitment:

[1] Billy Graham, *Peace With God* (Garden City, NY:Doubleday & Co., 1953), p.217.
[2] J. Vernon McGee, *Thru The Bible*, Vol.5, p.321.
[3] William Barclay, *The Letters to the Philippians, Colossians, and Thessalonians*, p.94.

	B. The Steps to Peace (Part II): Prayer & Positive Thinking, 4:6-9	8 Finally, brethren, whatsoever things are true, whatsoever things are honest, whatsoever things are just, whatsoever	2. Peace comes through positive thinking a. The charge: Think & do things that are...
1. Peace comes through prayer	6 Be careful for nothing; but in every thing	things are pure, whatsoever things are lovely,	1) True
a. The charge: Do not worry or be anxious	by prayer and supplication with thanksgiv-	whatsoever things are of good report; if there	2) Honest
b. The remedy: Prayer	ing let your requests	be any virtue, and if	3) Just
1) About everything	be made known unto	there be any praise,	4) Pure
2) With requests	God.	think on these things.	5) Lovely
3) With thanksgiving	7 And the peace of	9 Those things, which	6) Of good report
c. The promise: Peace	God, which passeth	ye have both learned,	7) Virtuous
1) Peace that passes all understanding	all understanding, shall keep your hearts and	and received, and heard, and seen in me, do:	8) Praise-worthy
2) Peace that keeps our hearts & minds	minds through Christ Jesus.	and the God of peace shall be with you.	b. The source or power of positive thinking
			1) The Word of God
			2) Noble examples
			3) Self-effort

Section V
THE SECRET OF PEACE:
THE PEACE OF GOD HIMSELF, Philippians 4:1-9

Study 2:   THE STEPS TO PEACE (PART II): PRAYER & POSITIVE THINKING

Text: Philippians 4:6-9

Aim: To learn to experience and keep the peace of God.

Memory Verse:
    "And the peace of God, which passeth all understanding, shall keep
    your hearts and minds through Christ Jesus" (Philippians 4:7).

INTRODUCTION:
    Have you ever tried to squeeze a wet bar of soap? It tends to shoot right out of your hands, doesn't it? It is kind of like the peace of God—one minute you think you have it and the next minute it's gone! But the problem isn't with the soap or with God's peace—the problem is with our grip. Is there a secret that could help us hold on to the peace of God—regardless of the circumstances? The answer is yes!

    Remember we are answering a question—once we possess the peace of God, how do we keep and maintain it? How do we keep the *peace of God* ruling and reigning within our hearts? How do we keep a consciousness of God's very own presence within us—an awareness that the "God of peace" lives within our very being? This passage discusses two of the most important steps to possessing peace. Above all other passages, it tells us how to have peace and how to maintain peace. If we will take these two steps, the peace of God will rule and reign in our hearts and lives.

OUTLINE:
    1.   Peace comes through prayer (v.6-7).
    2.   Peace comes through positive thinking (v.8-9).

1. PEACE COMES THROUGH PRAYER (v.6-7).

Note three significant points.
1.   There is the charge: be anxious about nothing (v.6). The idea is that the believer is not to worry or fret about a single thing. The word "nothing" means not even one thing. Humanly speaking, the Philippians had every reason to worry and be anxious.
⇒   They were suffering severe persecution (Ph.1:18-19).
⇒   They were facing a disturbance in the church, some disunity and quarreling (Ph.1:27, 42).
⇒   They had some carnal members within their fellowship, some members who were prideful, super-spiritual, and self-centered (Ph.2:3-4; 3:12).
⇒   They were facing some false teachers who had joined their fellowship, and the teachers were fierce in attacking the cross of Christ (Ph.3:2-3, 18-19).
⇒   Some of the believers were having to struggle for the necessities of life: food, clothing, and shelter (Ph.4:19).

There was little else that could confront these dear believers. They were facing about every trial and temptation imaginable, the kind of trouble that arouses anxiety and worry. Humanly, a person is going to fret, worry, and suffer anxiety...
•   when he is either about to lose or lacks food, clothing, or shelter.
•   when he is persecuted, ridiculed, abused, or threatened.
•   when he is surrounded by quarrels, disturbance, carnality, or false teaching.
In the midst of such circumstances, the only way a person can keep from worrying is to receive an injection of supernatural power.
This is the very point of Scripture. There is an answer to worry and anxiety, a supernatural answer: the peace of God. God will *enable* the believer to conquer worry and anxiety. God will overcome the trials of life for the believer, no matter how terrible and pressuring they may be. God will infuse the believer with peace—the very peace of God Himself—a peace so great and so wonderful that it carries the believer right through the trial. Of course, this does not mean the believer is not to be concerned about the problems of life. He is, but there is a difference between concern and anxiety or worry. Concern drives us to arise and tackle the problems of life with an indomitable courage and diligence. Concern drives us to tackle and conquer all that we can handle. Anxiety and worry cause all kinds of problems...

• fear to act	• quick, unplanned action
• withdrawal	• unwise and harmful decisions
• hesitation	• physical sickness and infirmities
• cowardice	• emotional problems
• depression	• spiritual backsliding
• discouragement	• distrust and unbelief
• a defeatist attitude	

Of course the list could go on and on, but the point to see is the seriousness of anxiety and worry. Just take a moment to think about a few of the above problems: how anxiety and worry cause a person to act and suffer. The seriousness is easily seen. We all know people who suffer greatly because of anxiety and worry; they simply lack the peace of God. Yet, the charge of Scripture is forceful: be anxious for nothing, not even for a single thing.

> **"Therefore take no thought, saying, What shall we eat? or, What shall we drink? or, Wherewithal shall we be clothed?...for your heavenly Father knoweth that ye have need of all these things. But seek ye first the kingdom of God, and his righteousness; and all these things shall be added unto you" (Mt.6:31-33).**

APPLICATION:
The first thing we need to do to achieve peace is turn our worry and anxiety into concern. Worry and anxiety are harmful and unproductive. Concern gets things done as we act on the problem with God's guidance.

QUESTIONS:
1. What kinds of things do you worry about?
2. When was the last time you solved a problem by worrying about it?
3. Think of something you are worried about right now. How can you act on it and allow God to help you through it?

2. The remedy for anxiety and worry: prayer. The four words used for prayer show exactly how prayer is the answer to anxiety and worry.
⇒ The word "prayer" refers to the special times of prayer that we share in periods of devotion and worship.
⇒ The word "supplication" refers to the prayers that focus upon special needs. We go before God and *supplicate*, that is, pour out our soul to God.
⇒ The word "thanksgiving" means that we thank and praise God for all that He is and for all that He has done for us.
⇒ The word "requests" means specific and definite requests. Our praying is not to be general, but specific. We are to lay before God exactly what is needed, and we are not to fear that we are being too detailed with God or bothering God. Too often believers fear not receiving the answer to a specific request, fear that it will show how weak they are spiritually if the request is not granted.

Note what Scripture says: "In everything" pray like this—use all four ways of praying and use them in praying for everything. This means two things.
a. We are to walk *with* God and *in* God, and we do this *by prayer*. We pray "in everything"—all day long as we walk and move about our daily affairs.
⇒ We *pray* in times that are specifically set aside for devotion and worship.
⇒ We *supplicate*—struggle in prayer—when facing times of deep and intense need.
⇒ We offer *thanksgiving* (and praise) all day long as we walk and move about.
⇒ We offer our *requests*—specific requests—to God. We ask Him to do definite things as we walk throughout the day.

b. We are to pray about everything no matter how small and insignificant it may seem. God is interested in the most minute details of our lives. He wants us acknowledging Him in *all our ways* because He wants to care for us and look after every single step.

Now picture the scene: we are walking throughout the day, sharing with God every step of the way, and God is taking care of every step we take. What then can take the peace of God away from us? Absolutely nothing! For as we walk in prayer and fellowship with God, God is infusing us with His presence and peace.
No matter the conflict or trial, we are continuing to share with God, and God is continuing to infuse us with His peace. Through prayer He is giving us the peace to conquer and walk through the trial. Our relationship with God and His peace is unbroken.

"Ask, and it shall be given you; seek, and ye shall find; knock, and it shall be opened unto you" (Mt.7:7).

1. When we are walking alone through a trial, has God deserted us or have we deserted Him?
2. Who or what do we have a tendency to turn to when we are worried about something? (Spouse, friend, co-worker, alcohol, drugs?) How can we shift our focus to seek God instead of others during these times?
3. When God instructs us to pray about everything, does He mean it literally? Does He really care about the insignificant details of our lives?
4. What are some things (details of life) that we should be praying about every day?

3.   The promise: peace. Peace means to be bound, joined, and woven together. It means to be secure in the love and care of God. It means to have a knowledge that God will...
- provide
- guide
- strengthen
- sustain
- deliver
- encourage
- save
- give real life both now and forever

A person can experience the peace of God only as he walks and moves about in prayer. Why? Because only God can *deliver man* through the most severe circumstances and tragedies of life; only God can *infuse assurance and security* within the human soul. The wonderful promise about the peace of God is twofold.
a.   First, the peace of God passes all understanding. It is beyond anything we can ask or think. It surpasses all our imaginations. Think of the most terrible situation you can imagine; then think of the peace you would want as you went through that trial. In actual experience, the peace of God is far greater than anything you could ever imagine or understand. The peace of God actually carries the faithful believer through the very midst of trial and tribulation.
b.   Second, the peace of God keeps our hearts and minds. The word "shall keep" is a military word meaning to guard and protect. The peace of God is like an elite soldier who guards and protects the most precious possession of God: the believer's heart and mind.

However, note that God can keep us only as we are "in Christ Jesus." We can know the peace of God only if we have trusted Christ as our Lord and Savior and only if we walk in fellowship with Him. To be in Christ means to walk in Christ—to live, move and have our being in Him.

> **"Peace I leave with you, my peace I give unto you: not as the world giveth, give I unto you. Let not your heart be troubled, neither let it be afraid" (Jn.14:27).**

ILLUSTRATION:
"Dr. A.C. Dixon of Spurgeon's Tabernacle once said....'When we rely upon organization, we get what organization can do, when we rely upon education, we get what education can do; when we rely upon eloquence, we get what eloquence can do....But...when we rely upon prayer, we get what God can do.'"[1]

When God answers our prayers, peace floods our hearts and lives. Anxiety is conquered and overcome.

1. What answer to prayer have you been waiting on? The salvation of a loved one...a situation at work...a broken relationship that needs to be healed? Are you continuing to pray about the situation? We must remember to enjoy God's peace as we wait for His answer!
2. How do you know for sure that you have God's peace? How would you explain your answer to a person who is not a Christian believer?

2. PEACE COMES THRU POSITIVE THINKING (v.8-9).

The word "think" means to consider, reflect, reason, and ponder. The idea is that of *focusing our thoughts until they shape our behavior.* The truth is:
⇒ what we think is what we become.
⇒ where we have kept our minds is where we are.
⇒ what we do is what we think.

A person who centers his thoughts upon the world and its things will live for the world and its things: money, wealth, lands, property, houses, possessions, position, power, recognition, honor, social standing, fame, and a host of other worldly pursuits. Very simply stated, a person who centers his thoughts...
- upon the flesh and its lusts will live to satisfy the flesh through such things as pride, self, greed, pleasure, and sex.
- upon the eyes and its lusts will live to satisfy the eyes and its lusts through such things as the immoral, pornographic filth flaunted in magazines, films, books, and television; the exposing of the human body; dressing to attract attention; looking a second time.
- upon the pride of life will live to satisfy such things as the desire for recognition, honor, position, and authority.

A mind focused upon the world and the flesh is what leads to anxiety and worry, emptiness and restlessness. A worldly mind never knows peace—not true peace, not the peace of God. God will just never allow a worldly mind to have peace, for it is the restlessness of the human soul that He uses to reach men for salvation.

Once a person has been converted to Christ and becomes a new man, he is to focus his thoughts upon the good things of life and upon God. He is to give his mind to *positive thinking.* In fact, he is to think only positive thoughts. The believer is never to allow an immoral, fleshly, worldly, selfish, sinful or evil thought to enter his mind. There is never to be a negative thought whatsoever in the mind of the believer. Sinful and negative thoughts disrupt and destroy peace. For this reason, the believer is to struggle to conquer his mind and thoughts. He is to exert every cell of energy possible to captivate and control every thought. What we think is so important that God tells us what we are to think.
1. The charge is to think and practice positive thinking.
   a. "Whatsoever things are *true*": real and genuine.
   b. "Whatsoever things are *honest*": honorable, worthy, revered, highly respected, and noble.
   c. "Whatsoever things are *just*": right and righteous behavior. It has to do with right behavior toward man and God.
   d. "Whatsoever things are *pure*": morally clean, spotless, undefiled, free from filth, dirt, and impurities.
   e. "Whatsover things are *lovely*": pleasing, kind, gracious; things that draw out love and kindness.
      The believer's thoughts are not to be thoughts of unkindness and meanness, grumbling and murmuring, criticism and reaction. The believer's thoughts are to be focused upon things that are lovely—that build people up, not tear them down.
   f. "Whatsoever things are of *good report*": reputable, worthy things; things of the highest quality.
      The believer is not to fill his mind with *bad reports*, no matter how *juicy* they man seem. Neither is he to fill his mind with junk, whether through rumor, radio, television, music, off-colored jokes, or by whatever source.
   g. "If there be any virtue [excellence] and if there be any praise [in any thought], think on these things." *Positive thinking is the answer to peace for the Christian believer.*

2. The source or power for positive thinking is twofold.
   a. There is the *Word of God*. Paul says that he had preached and taught the very virtues of positive thinking to the Philippians and that they had learned them. What Paul had preached and taught was the will of God; therefore, the source or power for positive thinking comes from the Word of God.

   > "All scripture is given by inspiration of God, and is profitable for doctrine, for reproof, for correction, for instruction in righteousness" (2 Tim.3:16).

   b. There are *noble examples*. Paul says that he lived as a testimony before the Philippians. Therefore, they could follow his example because he kept his thoughts and life upon the very virtues of positive thinking.

   > "Brethren be followers together of me, and mark them which walk so as ye have us for an ensample" (Ph.3:17).

3. There is the energy and power of self-effort and discipline. Note the words, "Those things...do." The believer is expected to...
   - control his mind
   - discipline his mind
   - struggle against all sinful and negative thoughts
   - fight to think only positive thoughts

Note the result of positive thinking: *the God of peace shall be with the believer*.

> "Thou wilt keep him in perfect peace, whose mind is stayed on thee" (Is.26:3).

APPLICATION:

As we begin to think positively about things, we will sense a peace that only God can give us—a peace that says:
   ⇒ "God will work all things out for good."
   ⇒ "God will make all things beautiful in His time."

We will sense a weight being lifted off our shoulders as we take our burdens to the Lord in prayer.

ILLUSTRATION:

Does "positive thinking" really made a difference? Listen to this statement:

> "'We do not advance upward unless we yearn upward,' it has been said. Our thoughts shape our lives. We grow little or big by the ideals we cherish and the thoughts upon which we dwell.
> "'Avoid worry, anger, fear, hate, and all abnormal and depressing mental states,' said an eminent authority on health. This victory over harmful thoughts cannot be achieved by suppressing these feelings, but by supplanting them with right thinking which is becoming to the followers of Jesus Christ, and which is the outgrowth of a close walk with the Lord,"[2]

QUESTIONS:
1. What kinds of worldly distractions compete for your mind?
2. Practice doesn't always make perfect, but it does make better. What kind of mental exercises can you do that will help you be a more positive thinker?

PHILIPPIANS 4:6-9

SUMMARY:

In this lesson, we have learned how to have the peace of God rule and reign in our lives. We have discovered that:

1. Peace comes through prayer.
2. Peace comes through positive thinking.

Now would be a good time to renew your commitment to the Lord Jesus by making room for Him in your busy life. Remember:
With His presence comes His peace.

PERSONAL JOURNAL NOTES:
(Reflection & Response)

1. The most important thing that I learned from this lesson was:

2. The area that I need to work on the most is:

3. I can apply this lesson to my life by:

4. Closing Statement of Commitment:

---

[1] *The European Harvest Field.* Quoted in *Three Thousand Illustrations for Christian Service,* p.500.

[2] *Gospel Herald.* Quoted in *Three Thousand Illustrations for Christian Service,* p.690.

VI. THE APPRECIATION FOR GOOD CHRISTIAN RELATIONSHIPS, 4:10-23

A. Appreciation: For a Church That Revives Its Sacrificial Giving, 4:10-19

1. Their giving was revived, & it flourished

10 But I rejoiced in the Lord greatly, that now at the last your care of me hath flourished again; wherein ye were also careful, but ye lacked opportunity.

2. Their giving was not necessary, but it was needed
   a. Giving is not necessary because God teaches contentment apart from circumstances

11 Not that I speak in respect of want: for I have learned, in whatsoever state I am, therewith to be content.
12 I know both how to be abased, and I know how to abound: every where and in all things I am instructed both to be full and to be hungry, both to abound and to suffer need.

   b. Giving is not nec-
   b. essary because Christ strengthens us through all

13 I can do all things through Christ which strengtheneth me.

   c. Giving is needed-- it is work well done

14 Notwithstanding ye have well done, that ye did communicate with my affliction.

3. Their giving was distinctive: They were the only church that gave, & they gave consistently

15 Now ye Philippians know also, that in the beginning of the gospel, when I departed from Macedonia, no church communicated with me as concerning giving and receiving, but ye only.
16 For even in Thessalonica ye sent once and again unto my necessity.

4. Their giving was sacrificial, & it was seen & rewarded by God
   a. God deposited fruit to their account

17 Not because I desire a gift: but I desire fruit that may abound to your account.

   b. God was well pleased

18 But I have all, and abound: I am full, having received of Epaphroditus the things which were sent from you, an odour of a sweet smell, a sacrifice acceptable, wellpleasing to God.

   c. God promised to supply all their need

19 But my God shall supply all your need according to his riches in glory by Christ Jesus.

Section VI:
THE APPRECIATION FOR GOOD CHRISTIAN RELATIONSHIPS,
Philippians 4:10-23

Study 1: **APPRECIATION: FOR A CHURCH THAT REVIVES ITS SACRIFICIAL GIVING**

Text: Philippians 4:10-19

Aim: To make a genuine pledge to Christ: To always give sacrificially.

Memory Verse:

"But my God shall supply all your need according to His riches in glory by Christ Jesus" (Ph 4:19).

PHILIPPIANS 4:10-19

INTRODUCTION:
Would you consider yourself to be a generous person—a giver? See if this shoe fits:

C.S. Lewis remarked:
> *"If our expenditure on comforts, luxuries, amusements, etc., [equal to] those with the same income as our own, we are probably giving away too little. If our charities do not at all pinch or hamper us...they are too small. There ought to be things we should like to do and cannot do becaue our charitable expenditure excludes them."*[1]

What does the Bible say about giving? A lot! This specific passage deals with stewardship, in particular the giving of money to meet the needs of ministers and missions or the spread of the gospel to the world. Remember: Paul is in prison facing the false charge of insurrection against the government. He is facing the death penalty if convicted. The Philippians had heard about his plight, and they had heard how Paul was standing fast and continuing to preach the gospel to everyone who visited him. The church was stirred to do two things: to take up a love offering and to send a man, Epaphroditus, to minister to Paul's needs.

This passage expresses Paul's appreciation for a church that is stirred to revive its interest in missions—stirred to begin giving *once again* to the support of God's ministers world-wide.

OUTLINE:
1. Their giving was revived, and it flourished (v.10).
2. Their giving was not necessary, but it was needed (v.11-14).
3. Their giving was distinctive: they were the only church that gave, and they gave consistently (v.15-16).
4. Their giving was sacrificial, and it was seen and rewarded by God (v.17-19).

1. THEIR GIVING WAS REVIVED & IT FLOURISHED (v.10).

Note the words "flourished again": it means to revive again. It is the picture of plants and flowers sprouting, shooting up, and blossoming *again*. The key word is *again*. When the church had been founded, the believers had supported Paul and his mission work on a regular basis. But for some reason they had dropped their mission support. That had probably been over ten to twelve years before. Why they had stopped sending support to Paul is not known. However, the point to see is the glorious revival of mission support that took place in the church. They picked up the support of Paul once again, and their giving flourished and blossomed anew. The joy and rejoicing of Paul's heart can just be imagined. He says, "I rejoiced in the Lord greatly."

APPLICATION 1:
Why had the church dropped its mission support of Paul? As stated, the reason is not known. In his gracious and kind way, Paul just passes over the issue by saying that he knew they cared for him, but they had just lacked opportunity to support him. Was their lack of support...
- legitimate: that is, due to persecution or poverty?
- illegitimate: that is, due to neglect and unconcern for the spread of the gospel and missions world-wide?

Being honest about the matter, it is difficult to conceive of a legitimate reason for dropping mission support. It is especially difficult to see a reason that would last as long as the ten to twelve years that the Philippian church had failed to support Paul. Whether legitimate or not, we all need to search our hearts about our own personal support of God's ministers and missions world-wide.
- ⇒ The gospel must be supported.
- ⇒ The gospel must be carried world-wide.
- ⇒ The need of the hour is for churches to awaken to the *world-wide mission* of Christ.
- ⇒ Ministers, missionaries, teachers, and evangelists—all of God's appointed preachers and teachers—must be supported as they carry the gospel to the world.

PHILIPPIANS 4:10-19

Note this: it has been many centuries since Jesus Christ came to die for the sins of men and to give them life. Yet, look at how little has been done—at how many have still not heard or believed the "good news."

⇒ Where are the laborers to carry the message? Where are those who actually pray for laborers as He instructed? Look at how many stay at home, and then look at the few out in the communities and fields of the world ministering and witnessing to the lost. Is this God's method? His will? Thought and honesty give us the answer. The problem is not that we do not know the truth. We know the truth: we know that we are to go. The problem is that we do not go. We are just unwilling to commit ourselves to go. We are unwilling to leave the comfort and security of our homes and offices, jobs and families to go into the communities and nations of the world.

But the need of the hour is for laborers—laborers who will do exactly what Christ commanded: **"Go ye into all the world, and preach the gospel to every creature" (Mk.16:15)**. And if we cannot go, then we must commit ourelves to support those who are willing to go!

> **"Therefore said he unto them, The harvest truly is great, but the labourers are few: pray ye therefore the Lord of the harvest, that he would send forth labourers into his harvest" (Lk.10:2).**

APPLICATION 2:
Think of your budget. Is the Lord's work a part of it? For most people, even Christians, putting aside money for the Lord's work is a difficult thing. It is such an easy thing to find something else to do with our money! But we must remember that it is only as we support the laborers that the gospel can be spread. Every person who spreads the gospel is a laborer and every field is a mission field.

ILLUSTRATION:
Do you give until it hurts or do you hurt when you give? Have you had a spiritual checkup lately? Listen carefully to this illustration:

> *"When you go to a doctor for your annual checkup, he or she will often begin to poke, prod, and press various places, all the while asking, 'Does it hurt? How about this?'*
> *"If you cry out in pain, one of two things has happened. Either the doctor has pushed too hard, without the right sensitivity, or, more likely, there's something wrong, and the doctor will say, 'We'd better do some more tests. It's not supposed to hurt there!'*
> *"So it is when ministers preach on financial responsibility, and certain members cry out in discomfort, criticizing the message and the messenger. Either the pastor has pushed too hard, or perhaps there's something wrong. In that case, I say, 'My friend, we're in need of the Great Physician because it's not supposed to hurt there.'"[2]*

QUESTIONS:
1. What is the most difficult thing for you to give? Money, material things, time, talents?
2. Where can you go to find out more about the missions programs and missionaries supported by your church?
3. Why is it important for the church, in addition to individuals, to support missions?

2. THEIR GIVING WAS NOT NECESSARY, BUT IT WAS NEEDED (v.11-14).
Very simply, what this means is that God will take care of His dear servant even if churches do not adequately care for him. Down through the centuries most churches have not adequately cared for their ministers. This is part of the sufferings most ministers have to bear in order to carry the gospel forth to a world reeling in desperate need. Yet, God's dear servants have gone forth despite whatever suffering they have had to bear. Note three significant points.
1. Giving is not *necessary* because God teaches His servants to be content, no matter the circumstances (v.11-12). The word "content" means to be satisfied; to be completely detached from circumstances. Note the word "learned." It was a learning experience. Paul had to learn to

from circumstances. Note the word "learned." It was a learning experience. Paul had to learn to conquer circumstances and not to let circumstances worry him. But note: he had learned contentment. He says three descriptive things:

⇒ he knew how to be abased (to live humbly with little) and how to abound (to live with plenty and prosperity).
⇒ he knew the *secret* to facing every situation, whether being full or going hungry.
⇒ he knew how to abound (live in plenty) and how to suffer need.

ILLUSTRATION:
Lehman Strauss says:

> "In those early days of my Christian experience I could not see how some Christians I knew could be content with so little of this world's goods. I sincerely trust that I am learning the secret. From what I see about me I do not hesitate to say that it is a secret many Christians have yet to learn. Paul needed to learn it. He said, 'I have learned....' The lesson of contentment was one he learned by degrees in varying circumstances. As a young unbelieving Jew, he had no want insofar as this world's possessions are concerned. He did not always know the divine provision of satisfaction, but after he was saved he came to learn it, not in the academic classroom, but as the result of a lengthy experience of trials and discipline, 'I have learned' is the language of a good student. Have you learned to be satisfied with your place and position and possessions in this life?"[3]

APPLICATION:
What was the secret Paul had learned? To be content regardless of circumstances.

"Not that I speak in respect of want: for I have learned, in what-soever state I am, therewith to be content" (Ph.4:11).

In many societies, the desire and drive to possess material goods has grown to the point of obsession. Men feel justified in doing whatever is necessary to get what they want. We must get back to the basics of being thankful and using what God has given us to help share the gospel.

QUESTIONS:
1. Why are some people, including some Christian believers, so materialistic minded?
2. What advantages will our possessions gain us when we face our Lord?
3. What can we do to lead our home, church, and community to give sacrificially and willingly?

2. Giving is not necessary because the minister can do all things through Christ who strengthens him (v.13). Note the verse:

"I can do all things through Christ which strengtheneth me" (Ph.4:13).

God's servant can be content in all circumstances no matter how severe they are—through Christ—but *the servant cannot be content in any circumstance apart from Christ.* Note exactly what the verse says:
⇒ "I can...through Christ"
⇒ "Christ who strengthens me"

Christ does not do everything for the believer; neither does the believer do everything for himself. Both Christ and the believer have a part in conquering circumstances. The believer declares, "I can," and he gets up to face the circumstances head on. It is then that Christ steps in to strengthen the believer. Christ infuses strength into the believer *while the believer* is tackling the problem.

It is only when the believer has exhausted what he can do that a *special infusion* of the strength of Christ is needed. Christ steps in when our strength is no longer sufficient. It is then that He is able to demonstrate His wonderful love and care for His dear servant. Note something else as well: all praise and glory is then due Christ and not man. Giving is not necessary; God will provide and care for His dear servant.

> **"And he said unto me, My grace is sufficient for thee: for my strength is made perfect in weakness" (2 Cor.12:9).**

3. However, giving is needed, and it is work well done (v.14). The minister needs daily provision, and the gospel needs to be supported so that it can be carried around the world. Money and support are greatly needed. As stated before, they are not necessary; God can take care of His dear servants and the gospel with or without any church. But His will is for every single church to become involved in supporting His servants and world-wide missions. God can do the job without us; God can bypass us and put us on the shelf just like a useless book. But He wants His people to give and to give generously. When they do, they perform a work that is well done, that is commendable and noble.

> **"I have showed you all things how that so labouring ye ought to support the weak, and to remember the words of the Lord Jesus, how he said, It is more blessed to give than to receive" (Acts 20:35).**

ILLUSTRATION:
Do you control your money or does your money control you? Bill Hybles shares this personal story:

> *"When I left the family business to enter the ministry, I turned down a golden opportunity for affluence, I say that with no credit to myself. I felt God's call so definitely that I simply could not refuse. For two years I ministered with no salary. Lynne (his wife) taught music lessons and we took in borders to cover the rent. Then I began receiving thirty-five dollars a week, and later eighty-five. We were thrilled!.*
>
> *"Eventually our salary was set at twelve thousand dollars a year. I remember thinking, "Who would ever want more than twelve thousand dollars a year? Soon I found the answer. Me.*
>
> *"As the church grew and my job description enlarged, the board of directors periodically increased my salary. Each time I thought, "Wow, this is far more than I need. Who would ever want more than this? Twelve months later, I would find out. Me.*
>
> *"Finally, in a late night truth-telling session, I came to grips with an ugly reality. The more I had, the more I wanted. I'd been believing the Money Monster's lie that just a little bit more would be enough. But when would the drive to accumulate stop? Lynne and I decided then and there to cap my salary. The board agreed to our request, and helped us strike a deadly blow to the Money Monster."[4]*

APPLICATION:
In the above illustration, the man was...
- alert enough to recognize the problem.
- honest enough to admit the problem.
- brave enough to do something about the problem.
- trusting enough to turn the problem over the Lord.

QUESTIONS:
1. How many people today would be so daring as to turn down a raise in order to hold their spending down?
2. But should our income have a bearing on whether we give to support the spread of the gospel?

3. Whose giving will be blessed more by the Lord: the man who makes $100,000 a year and gives $10,000, or the man who makes $10,000 a year and gives $1000?
4. Why is it important for you to give to the Lord's work?
5. Do you give in order to get? Why?

3. THEIR GIVING WAS DISTINCTIVE: THEY WERE THE ONLY CHURCH THAT GAVE, & THEY GAVE CONSISTENTLY (v.15-16).

This is a point that desperately needs to be heeded by churches everywhere. When the Philippian church was founded, it underwrote the ministry of Paul, and it was consistent in its support. But note: it was the only church that was supporting Paul. The unfaithfulness of the other churches cut Paul's heart. This is clear from his words that no church supported him—none except the Philippian church.

It was while he was in Thessalonica that the Philippians had been consistent in their mission support. And how he had needed their support in Thessalonica, for it was there that he had faced severe persecution (cp. Acts 17:1f).

APPLICATION:

Imagine! Just one church supporting Paul and his mission to the world! And that church was a church that had just been founded. Two questions desperately need to be asked by all of us.
1. What are we doing for the Pauls and missions of today?
2. Have we made a commitment to support some minister or mission and backed off the commitment?

> "And the cares of this world, and the deceitfulness of riches, and the lusts of other things entering in, choke the word, and it becometh unfruitful" (Mk.4:19).

Note this truth: we usually find time and resources for our passions. Maybe we need to refocus our passions!

QUESTIONS:
1. Examine your passions. On a scale of 1 (low) to 10 (high), score yourself on the following items:
      Worshipping God
      Personal Bible Study & Prayer
      Sharing Christ Consistently
      Fellowship With Other Believers
      Prayer Meetings
      Missions Support
      Becoming Financially Wealthy
      Meeting All Of My Needs & Wants
      Avoiding Any Suffering
2. Based on the above, what changes do you need to make? Why?

4. THEIR GIVING WAS SACRIFICIAL, AND IT WAS SEEN & REWARDED BY GOD (v.17-19).

The gift cost the Philippian church. They were a church that gave, not just a percentage (so to speak) but sacrificially. This is seen in two points. Their gift is said to be a definite *sacrifice*, acceptable and well pleasing to God. Their gift is also said to have created a *need* among themselves. But Paul answers them, "God shall supply all your needs...." (v.19). Note three points.
1. God saw who sacrificially gave to support Paul, and He deposited a reward to their account (v.17). This was what Paul desired in giving: not a gift for himself but a reward for the

giver. Paul knew that God saw and rewarded the believers who gave sacrificially; therefore, Paul desired believers to give sacrificially.

> **"But lay up for yourselves treasures in heaven, where neither moth nor rust doth corrupt, and where thieves do not break through nor steal" (Mt.6:20).**

2. God was well pleased with the giving of the Philippians (v.18). Paul compares it to an Old Testament sacrifice which a person offered up to God. The person's sacrificial commitment to God was just like the *pleasant smell* of the animal sacrifice: it was acceptable. The sacrificial commitment was a sweet or pleasant smell to God. So it was and is with sacrificial giving. The commitment of the gift is acceptable to God just like the pleasant smell of an animal sacrifice.

> **"But I have all, and abound: I am full, having received of Epaphroditus the things which were sent from you, an odour of a sweet smell, a sacrifice acceptable, wellpleasing to God" (Ph.4:18).**

3. God promised to supply all the needs of His dear people (v.19). This is one of the great promises of Scripture:

> **"But my God shall supply all your need according to his riches in glory by Christ Jesus" (Ph.4:19).**

a. There is the great *Provider*: *God Himself*. No matter what the need is, the need is not greater than God. God can and will meet the need. But note the pronoun "my." It is "my God" who shall provide for the needs. A person has to make sure...
   • that the God who can really provide for needs *is his God*.
   • that *he knows God personally*—well enough that he can trust and depend upon God to meet his need.

b. There is the great *assurance* of provision: "my God shall supply." There is no question about the provision being supplied. God is God; therefore, He is able to provide, and He will supply whatever provision His dear child needs.

c. There is the great *provision*: "all your needs." This promise does not refer only to the physical needs for food, clothing, and shelter. It refers to mental, emotional, social, and spiritual needs. It refers to any need that arises, engulfs, or confronts the believer. No need will be omitted or overlooked. No need is too big or too little. No need is unimportant—not to God, not if His dear child is really experiencing the need.
   ⇒ There may be a lesson for the believer to learn before the need can be met, some lesson such as more trust, endurance, love, joy, peace, gentleness, meekness, or control.
   ⇒ There may be some testimony that the believer needs to share, a testimony that proclaims the strength of Christ to carry us through all trials.
   But no matter what the trial or need is, God will supply all our needs.

d. There is the great *resource*: "according to His riches in glory." Take all the riches and wealth, glory and majesty of heaven—it is all available to meet the needs of God's dear people. There is no limit to the great resources at God's disposal. God can provide for any need.

e. There is the great *Mediator*: "by Christ Jesus." This is critical to note, for God does nothing apart from Christ. No person can approach God without coming to Him through Christ Jesus. This is the key to having our needs met: surrendering our lives to Jesus Christ, and asking God to meet our needs *in Him*. We must always remember that God has only one begotten Son: the Lord Jesus Christ. God loves Christ so much that He will do anything for the person who honors Christ by sacrificially giving to share the glorious news about Him.

PHILIPPIANS 4:10-19

"And God is able to make all grace abound toward you; that ye, always having all sufficiency in all things, may abound to every good work" (2 Cor.9:8).

<u>**QUESTIONS:**</u>
1. Are you giving sacrificially in order to meet the needs of people and to spread the gospel around the world? If not, why not?
2. Why do so many believers not give sacrificially?
3. If you give sacrificially, God has promised to meet all your needs. What is your definition of "needs"? Are these needs the same for everyone?
4. Has God promised to give you your "wants"? Explain your answer.
5. What should be your motivation in giving?

<u>**SUMMARY:**</u>

In this lesson, we have learned Christian principles of stewardship, particularly with regards to the giving of money to meet the needs of the gospel ministry.
1. Our giving must be revived and flourish.
2. Our giving is not necessary, but it is needed.
3. We must give and give consistently.
4. Our sacrificial giving will be seen and rewarded by God.

Are you giving sacrificially? Think of the words of this famous hymn, *I Gave My Life For Thee*:

"I gave My life for thee, My precious blood I shed,
That thou might'st ransomed be, And quickened from the dead;
I gave, I gave My life for thee, What hast thou given for Me?" (Text By: Frances R. Havergal).

PERSONAL JOURNAL NOTES:
(Reflection & Response)

1. The most important thing that I learned from this lesson was:

2. The area that I need to work on the most is:

3. I can apply this lesson to my life by:

4. Closing Statement of Commitment:

[1] R. Kent Hughes, *Disciplines of a Godly Man* (Wheaton, IL: Crossway Books, 1991), p.179.
[2] Craig B. Larson, Editor, *Illustrations for Preaching and Teaching*, p.157.
[3] Lehman Strauss, *Devotional Studies in Philippians*, p.321.
[4] Bill Hybles, *Honest to God?* (Grand Rapids, MI: Zondervan, 1990), p.154

	B. Appreciation: For God & For Fellow Christians, 4:20-23
1. God is to be praised as God & as our Father	20 Now unto God and our Father be glory for ever and ever. Amen.
2. Believers are to salute every saint	21 Salute every saint in Christ Jesus. The
a. Christian leaders are to greet every saint	brethren which are with me greet you.
b. All the saints are to greet other believers, including government officials	22 All the saints salute you, chiefly they that are of Caesar's household.
3. Believers are to wish the grace of our Lord Jesus Christ upon each other	23 The grace of our Lord Jesus Christ be with you all. Amen.

Section VI
THE APPRECIATION FOR GOOD CHRISTIAN RELATIONS,
Philippians 4:10-23

Study 2:   APPRECIATION: FOR GOD & FOR FELLOW CHRISTIANS

Text: Philippians 4:20-23

Aim: To more actively express our appreciation (praise) to God and to fellow believers.

Memory Verse:
   "**The grace of our Lord Jesus Christ be with you all. Amen**" (Ph.4:23).

INTRODUCTION:
   "Johnny, What do you say?" Or "Johnny, say Thank You!" How many times have you said this as a parent or heard this as a child when receiving a gift or compliment or some act of care and love from someone? Thanking people for being kind and good is ingrained in us, and it should be.

   Paul and the Philippian believers had many memories of such acts. Appreciation for God and for each other was very much in order. But note: it is just as important for believers in this generation to express their love and appreciation for each other as it was for Paul and the Philippian believers. Too often we just take things for granted and go about our business without saying a word of thanks to others. Too often we allow our own concerns to get in the way of our being gracious, thankful, and appreciative. This passage gives us a dynamic challenge. We should be far more active in expressing appreciation to God and to fellow believers.

OUTLINE:
1.   God is to be praised as God and as our Father (v.20).
2.   Believers are to salute every saint (v.21-22).
3.   Believers are to wish the grace of our Lord Jesus Christ upon each other (v.23).

1. GOD IS TO BE PRAISED AS GOD AND AS OUR FATHER (v.20).

1.   First, God is to be praised as the Creator and Sovereign Ruler of the universe. God has made all, and He rules and governs all.

He is the only wise God...
- who dwells in majesty and glory, dominion and power (Jude 24-25).
- who possesses the bottomless depth of wisdom and knowledge.
- who possesses all the riches of wisdom and knowledge.

He is the One...
- whose judgments are unsearchable.
- whose ways are past finding out.
- who has a mind that no man can know.
- who has such wisdom that no man can be a counsellor to Him: "For of Him, and through Him, and to Him, are all things: to whom be glory for ever. Amen" (Ro.11:36).
- who reigns and is clothed with majesty and strength, whose very voice is the embodiment of power and of creation (Ps.29:4; 93:1; 96:6).
- whose glory is like a devouring fire (Ex.24:17).
- whose glory is declared by the heavens, and whose handiwork is shown by the firmament (Ps.19:1).

2.   God is to be praised as *our Father*. Imagine! The Sovereign Majesty of the universe has humbled Himself so much that He has adopted us as His sons and daughters. Just think about the fact. He is the Sovereign Power not only of this earth, but of the whole universe. Yet...
- we have criticized, grumbled, and complained about His rule.
- we have cursed His very name.
- we have rebelled and rejected Him.
- we have questioned and denied Him, and even scoffed at the very idea of Him.
- we have deliberately disobeyed Him.
- we have chosen to live as we please and to do our own thing instead of following Him.

Just think about our attitude and behavior toward God. Yet, He has not wiped us out; He has not destroyed us. On the contrary, He has sent His Son into the world to declare that He loves the world and that He wants to reconcile us to Himself. How? Through the death of His Son Jesus Christ. God wants to adopt men and women as sons and daughters through faith in the death of His Son.

This is *the great humility (or condescension) and mercy* of God—that He, as the Sovereign Ruler of the universe whom we have rejected and cursed so much, would still save and adopt us and let us call Him Father.

The great condescension of God demands one thing: that we praise and glorify Him *as our Father for ever and ever.*

> **"For ye have not received the spirit of bondage again to fear; but ye have received the Spirit of adoption, whereby we cry, Abba, Father. The Spirit itself beareth witness with our spirit, that we are the children of God: and if children, then heirs; heirs of God, and jointheirs with Christ; if so be that we suffer with him, that we may be also glorified together" (Ro.8:15-17).**

APPLICATION:
Think of the modern-day heroes of any generation. Think about their qualities and the factors that made them famous or popular: good looks, sex appeal, acting ability, great wealth, athletic ability, and on and on. All of these characteristics are only temporary—here today and gone tomorrow. Age, loss of looks, disability, and loss of fortune will quickly devastate anyone who is counting on the physical things of this world

to carry them through life. None of the things which they hold in such high esteem will gain them another day of life or even guarantee them happiness. The bottom line is that no person and no thing is deserving of our praise, honor, and worship. God alone is the Creator and Sustainer of the universe; He alone is deserving of our worship. We owe Him for our very life and we owe Him for adopting us as His children through the blood of His Son, Jesus Christ. We owe Him for our eternity!

QUESTIONS:
1. Why should God be praised?
2. In what ways is your heavenly Father different from your earthly father?

2. BELIEVERS ARE TO SALUTE EVERY SAINT (v.21-22).

"Saint" means those who are separated or set apart unto God; those who are different from the person who lives for the world, for its possessions and pleasures. Note: every saint is to be greeted. There is to be no discrimination or favoritism shown. Among saints there is to be...

• no clique	• no neglect	• no sense of pride
• no ignoring	• no snubbing	• no sense of superiority
• no downgrading	• no separation	• no sense of super-
• no withdrawal	• no avoiding	spirituality

Poverty, education, handicap, unattractiveness, clothing, social standing, employment, race, nationality—nothing is to cause believers to discriminate or to show partiality and favoritism. All saints are equally acceptable to God.

1. *Christian leaders are to greet every saint*. Note that "all the brothers" with Paul send their greetings. This apparently refers to the ministers who accompanied and served with Paul in his ministry—men such as Timothy and Luke. The point to note is that the *Christian leaders* are to take the lead in greeting *every saint*. If the leader shows discrimination and favoritism, then others in the church will do the same. The minister and other leaders must always demonstrate love, interest, and care *for all*.

2. *All the saints, including government officials, are to greet every saint*. Caesar's household does not necessarily refer to members of Caesar's family. The term is very similar to what we call civil servants, or government employees. As in our day, Rome had its government employees scattered all over the world. But note: Paul was in Rome, so this means that some government officials had been reached for Christ. The lesson for us is that humility must be demonstrated even by those in the echelons of government, no matter how high their position is. Even if a person is in Caesar's household, in the highest position of government, he must walk humbly before God and greet all the saints, even the lowest saint.

> **"Let nothing be done through strife or vainglory; but in lowliness of mind let each esteem other better than themselves. Look not every man on his own things, but every man also on the things of others"** (Ph.2:3-4).

ILLUSTRATION:
There is never to be discrimination and prejudice between believers. We are to greet every believer as a saint, as a true believer in our Lord Jesus Christ. The true brotherhood of believers was graphically demonstrated in the following event:

> *"A Hindu and a New Zealander met upon the deck of a missionary ship. They had been converted from their heathenism, and were brothers in Christ, but they could not speak to each other. They pointed to their Bibles, shook hands, and smiled in each other's face; but that was all. At last a happy thought occurred to the Hindu. With sudden joy, he exclaimed, 'Hallelujah!' The New Zealander, in*

delight, cried out, 'Amen!' Those two words, not found in their own heathen tongues, were to them the beginning of 'one language and one speech.'"[1]

As stated, all believers are brothers and sisters in Christ. No matter our nationality or social status, we are to greet and open our hearts, homes, and churches to one another.

QUESTIONS:
1. What are some ways you can greet and express appreciation to other believers?
2. All of the ground at the foot of the cross is level. Who do you know in your church who is having a hard time fitting in? What special effort can you make to help them feel included?

3. BELIEVERS ARE TO WISH THE GRACE OF OUR LORD JESUS CHRIST UPON EACH OTHER (v.23).

Paul ends his message to this great church with a strong command: share the wonderful grace of God with each other.

What an incredible privilige we have! God has entrusted each believer with the priceless grace of God. It is a grace that gives hope to the hopeless; joy to the sorrowful; peace to the anxious; and help to the helpless.

We must not hoard God's grace. His grace must be shared with the world around us. We must be a channel of God's grace to the world.

ILLUSTRATION:
R.G. Le Tourneau, a wealthy businessman, was a great lay witness for our Lord. This was his challenge to laymen:

"My challenge to laymen is [this]: when Christ said, 'Go ye into all the world, and preach the Gospel,' He did not mean only preachers but everyone who believed on Him as the Lord of Glory. The division between the clergy and the laity is a division of our own making...[it] was not instituted by Christ, nor was it evidenced in the early Church. They believed the word 'Go' meant every man, and they obeyed the Lord's command. My challenge to you is for a return to this first century...Christianity where every believer is a witness to the grace of the Lord Jesus Christ."

QUESTIONS:
1. How has God favored you, showered His grace upon you? What kinds of things has He done for you?
2. Who can you share God's grace with today, this week?

SUMMARY:

It is crucial that we worship God properly and learn to do a better job of appreciating other believers. Remember, we must:
1. Praise God as God and as our Father.
2. Salute every saint.
3. Wish the grace of our Lord Jesus Christ upon each other.

It would be very appropriate to close this study with some thoughts from the great hymn *"Wonderful Grace of Jesus"*:

Wonderful grace of Jesus, Greater than all my sin;
How shall my tongue describe it, Where shall its praise begin?
Taking away my burden, Setting my spirit free,
For the wonderful grace of Jesus reaches me.[3]

PERSONAL JOURNAL NOTES:
(Reflection & Response)

1. The most important thing that I learned from this lesson was:

2. The area that I need to work on the most is:

3. I can apply this lesson to my life by:

4. Closing Statement of Commitment:

---

[1] *Gospel Herald,* Quoted in *Three Thousand Illustrations for Christian Service*, p.279.
[2] R.G. Le Tourneau, Quoted in *Three Thousand Illustrations for Christian Service*, p.724-725.
[3] Words and music by Haldor Lillenas (Carol Stream, IL: Hope Publishing Company, 1946).

OUTLINE & SUBJECT INDEX

PHILIPPIANS

OUTLINE & SUBJECT INDEX

Philippians

REMEMBER: When you look up a subject and turn to the Scripture reference, you have not only the Scripture, you also have an outline and a discussion (commentary) of the Scripture and subject.

This is one of the GREAT VALUES of *The Teacher's Outline & Study Bible*. Once you have all the volumes, you will have not only what all other Bible indexes give you, that is, a list of all the subjects and their Scripture references, BUT you will also have...

- An outline of every Scripture and subject in the Bible.
- A discussion (commentary) on every Scripture and subject.
- Every subject supported by other Scriptures or cross references.

DISCOVER THE GREAT VALUE for yourself. Quickly glance below to one of the very first subjects of the Index of Philippians. It is:

APPRECIATION
    For what.
        Good Christian relationships.   Ph.4:10-23

Turn to the reference. Glance at the Scripture and outline of the Scripture, then read the commentary. You will immediately see the GREAT VALUE of the INDEX of The Teacher's Outline & Study Bible.

OUTLINE AND SUBJECT INDEX

APPRECIATION
For what.
    Good Christian relationships.   Ph.4:10-23
    A church that revives its sacrificial giving.   Ph.4:10-19
    God & for fellow Christians.   Ph.4:20-23

ASSURANCE (See **CARE--CARING; CHURCH; SECURITY**)
Comes by.
        God's keeping power.   Ph.1:6
        God's supply.   Ph.4:17-19
        Prayer.   Ph.4:6-7
Of Salvation.   Ph.1:6; 1:19
Source.
        God. He will complete the work He began.   Ph.1:6

OUTLINE & SUBJECT INDEX

OUTLINE & SUBJECT INDEX

OUTLINE & SUBJECT INDEX

OUTLINE & SUBJECT INDEX

OUTLINE & SUBJECT INDEX

OUTLINE & SUBJECT INDEX

OUTLINE & SUBJECT INDEX

OUTLINE & SUBJECT INDEX

OUTLINE & SUBJECT INDEX

OUTLINE & SUBJECT INDEX

OUTLINE & SUBJECT INDEX

OUTLINE & SUBJECT INDEX

SCRIPTURE INDEX

PHILIPPIANS

SCRIPTURE INDEX

(The Scripture Index follows the Order of the Books of the Bible)

	Page		Page		Page
Genesis		**Matthew**		**Luke**	
15:2	65	1:20-22	65	1:43	65
17:10-14	92	2:15	65	1:68	65
32:28	96	3:3	65	2:9	65
		4:7	65	9:23	29, 73, 101
Exodus		4:10	65	9:23-24	39, 84
24:17	140	4:11	65	10:2	133
		4:25	65	12:15	111
Numbers		5:14	72	13:24	104
20:2f.	71	5:20	98	15:7	25
21:4	71	5:48	105	24:47	64
		6:10	24		
Judges		6:11	24	**John**	
5:14	97	6:13	24	1:1	60
		6:14-15	122	1:12	81
1 Samuel		6:20	137	3:3	92
17:26, 36	92	6:31-33	125	3:16	40
		7:7	126	4:23-24	91
2 Samuel		7:11	24	6:63	70
1:20	92	7:12	40	10:10	72
		7:15	89	10:18	62
1 Kings		7:21	65	10:30	61
12:1	97	8:2	65	12:26	17
		10:28	69	13:34-35	28, 52
		11:29	55	14:2-3	41
Psalms		12:8	65	14:8-10	65
5:11	25, 88	16:26	57	14:16	26
51:10	72	18:3-4	55	14:18	51
16:11	25	18:15-20	120	14:27	127
19:1	140	18:20	26	14:27	20
29:4	140	19:21	77	14:28	25
93:1	140	20:28	82	15:11	25, 54
96:6	140	21:9	65	15:13-14	82
		22:43-45	65	15:20	48
Isaiah		22:44	65	16:23-24	64
1:18	72	23:12	55	16:24	25
26:3	129	24:44	42, 113	17:5	62
		25:23	41	17:13	25
Jeremiah		25:43	56	20:21	40
3:15	76	26:39	101	20:28	65
31:34	105	26:42	101	21:21-22	35
		28:19-20	28		
Hosea				**Acts**	
5:8	97	**Mark**		4:20	31
		4:19	136	6:8	19
Micah		10:28	100	8:5	19
7:19	105	10:43-44	19	9:5	65
		12:29-30	65	10:1	92
		16:15	34, 133	16:1	78

SCRIPTURE INDEX

SCRIPTURE INDEX

	Page		Page		Page
Titus		**James**		**1 John**	
2:10	46	5:13	24	1:3-4	25
		5:16	24	2:28	38, 106
Hebrews					
1:3	60	**1 Peter**		**3 John**	
8:12	105	1:20	92	1:4	25
10:10	18	3:15	73		
10:17	105	4:14	101	**Jude**	
10:34	25			24-25	140
11:6	99	**2 Peter**			
12:2	25	1:4	92	**Revelation**	
		3:10-12	18	15:4	64

ILLUSTRATION INDEX

PHILIPPIANS

ILLUSTRATION INDEX

ILLUSTRATION INDEX

ILLUSTRATION INDEX

PURPOSE STATEMENT

LEADERSHIP MINISTRIES WORLDWIDE
exists to equip ministers, teachers, and laymen in their
understanding, preaching, and teaching of God's Word
by publishing and distributing worldwide
The Preacher's Outline & Sermon Bible™
and related *Outline* Bible materials,
to reach & disciple men, women, boys, and girls for Jesus Christ.

• MISSION STATEMENT •

1. To make the Bible so understandable - its truth so clear and plain - that men
   and women everywhere, whether teacher or student, preacher or hearer,
   can grasp its Message and receive Jesus Christ as Savior; and...
2. To place the Bible in the hands of all who will preach and teach God's Holy
   Word, verse by verse, precept by precept, regardless of the individual's
   ability to purchase it.

The *Outline* Bible materials have been given to LMW for printing and especially
distribution worldwide at/below cost, by those who remain anonymous. One fact,
however, is as true today as it was in the time of Christ:

• The Gospel is free, but the cost of taking it is not •

LMW depends on the generous gifts of Believers with a heart for Him and a love and
burden for the lost. They help pay for the printing, translating, and placing *Outline*
Bible materials in the hands and hearts of those worldwide who will present God's
message with clarity, authority and understanding beyond their own.

LMW was incorporated in the state of Tennessee in July 1992 and received IRS 501(c) 3 non-
profit status in March 1994. LMW is an international, nondenominational mission organization.
All proceeds from USA sales, along with donations from donor partners, go 100% into under-
writing our translation and distribution projects of *Outline* Bible materials to preachers,
church & lay leaders, and Bible students around the world.

PO Box 21310 - Chattanooga, TN 37424 - (615) 855-2181 — FAX (615) 855-8616

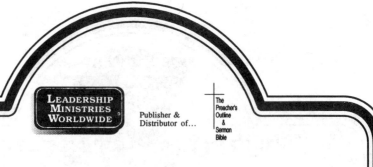

LEADERSHIP MINISTRIES WORLDWIDE

Publisher & Distributor of...

The Preacher's Outline & Sermon Bible

Sharing the OUTLINED BIBLE with the World!

1. **AUTO-PLAN.** Your automatic monthly way to get any/all the volumes, paying as you go.

2. **NEW TESTAMENT.** Compete in 14 volumes. You get a FREE Volume when you purchase the Full Set altogether, or through **Auto-Plan.**

3. **OLD TESTAMENT.** In process; 1 volume releases about every 6-8 months, in sequence.

4. **THE MINISTERS HANDBOOK.** Acclaimed as a "must-have" for every minister. Outlines more than 400 verses into topics like Power, Victory, Encouragement, Security, Restoration, plus more than 100 others. Discount for quantities.

5. *THE TEACHER'S OUTLINE & STUDY BIBLE.* Verse-by-verse study & teaching; 45 minute lesson or session. Ideal for study, small groups, classes, even home schooling. Student takeaway at cost. New Testament will be 42± vols.

6. **CD-ROM.** Fall 1995. Complete NT, Master Index, Minister's Handbook. Both Windows 3.1 & Macintosh. Includes KJV, NIV, NASB, M.Henry, J.Gill, Eastons Dictionary, Vine's & others are just some of the helpful works included on this Electronic Biblical Workshop. Outstanding!

7. **THE *OUTLINE.*** Quarterly newsletter to all users and owners of *POSB.* Complimentary.

8. **LMW AGENT PLAN.** An exciting way any user sells *OUTLINE* materials & earns a second income.

9. **DISTRIBUTION.** Our ultimate mission is to provide *POSB* volumes & materials to preachers, pastors, national church leaders around the world. This is especially for those unable to purchase at U.S. price. USA sales gain goes 100% to provide volumes at affordable prices within the local economy.

10. **TRANSLATIONS.** Korean, Russian, & Spanish are shipping first volumes — a great effort and expense. Next priority: Mandarin Chinese (1996) with 6 other languages awaiting funding.

11. **FUNDING PARTNERS.** To cover the cost of all the translations, plus print, publish, and distribute around the world is a multi million dollar project. However, as thousands of partners generously respond from willing hearts, we're confident God will supply the funds and other needs.

12. **REFERRALS.** Literally thousands (perhaps even you!) first heard of *POSB* from a fellow preacher, minister, or friend — Word of mouth from excited users is the way. *Please tell someone Today!*

13. **CURRICULUM & COPYRIGHT.** Permission may be given to copy specific portions of *POSB* for special group situations. Write for details.

Please PRAY 1 Minute/Day for LMW!

PO Box 21310, Chattanooga, TN 37424 — (615) 855-2181 — FAX (615) 855-8616

LEADERSHIP
MINISTRIES
WORLDWIDE

The
Preacher's
Outline
&
Sermon
Bible

Sharing

The

OUTLINED

BIBLE

With the World!